Carnegie Endowment National Commission on America and the New World

S0-BNR-261

Carnegie
Endowment
National
Commission
on America
and the
New World

Carnegie
Endowment for
International
Peace
National
Commission

Changing Our Ways

America

and the

New World

Great care for the environment was exercised in the design and
production of this report. It is 100% recyclable, contains 75%
recycled paper and is printed with soy-based inks.

Design: The Invisions Group Ltd.
Copy Editor: Sharon Block
Printing: Peake Printers, Inc.
Cover Earth Image: Weststock
Cover Handmade Paper: Alan Potash
Photography: Karen Holzberg

For information regarding sales of this book, please contact:
Brookings Institution
1775 Massachusetts Avenue, N.W.
Washington, D.C. 20036
202-797-6258
Toll-Free 1-800-275-1447

Library of Congress Cataloging-in-Publication Data

Changing Our Ways : America and the New World / Carnegie Endowment
    National Commission on America and the New World.
        p.   cm.
    ISBN 0 87003-034-5 : $9.95
    1. United States–Foreign relations–1989- I. Carnegie Endowment
National Commission on America and the New World.
E881.C46 1992
327.73–dc20   92-27961
                                    CIP

I. The New Landscape

This is the time for us to change the way we think about the world and the way we conduct our affairs at home and abroad. _(p.1)

Today foreign policy can raise or lower the cost of your home mortgage, create a new job or cause you to lose the one you've got. _(p.2)

Leadership must be of a new kind – one that mobilizes collective action; few great goals can be reached without America, but America can no longer reach many of them alone. _(p.4)

This is the time for us to change the way we think about the world and the way we conduct our affairs at home and abroad. (p.1)

Today foreign policy can raise or lower the cost of your home mortgage, create a new job or cause you to lose the one you've got. (p.2)

Leadership must be of a new kind – one that mobilizes collective action; few great goals can be reached without America, but America can no longer reach many of them alone. (p.4)

II. New Priorities

To advance our interests abroad we must get our own house in order. An America that lacks economic strength and social cohesion will lose respect abroad. (p.7)

Our government may be broke, but our country is not poor.... Our crisis is essentially political, not economic. (p.8)

Our leaders will have to put the national interest ahead of their own careers. They must accept the burden of explanation that goes with their election to high office. (p.8)

To advance our interests abroad we must get our own house in order. An America that lacks economic strength and social cohesion will lose respect abroad. (p.7)

Our government may be broke, but our country is not poor....
Our crisis is essentially political, not economic. (p.8)

Our leaders will have to put the national interest ahead of their own careers. They must accept the burden of explanation that goes with their election to high office. (p.8)

Hundreds of millions of people are born each
year into a world of deprivation and desperation
unimaginable to most Americans. (p.30)

The present system needs a
fundamental overhaul. (p.34)

Greater economic parity among North America, East Asia
and Europe has caused a sea change in world trade and finance.
We have no choice but to move from what was formerly the
hegemony of a single country to collective management by the
industrial democracies. (p.36)

The Commission strongly endorses a major U.S. commitment to the successful
transition of the former Soviet bloc. We have taken on such a challenge before and
been the better for it. (p.33)

Hundreds of millions of people are born each year into a world of deprivation and desperation unimaginable to most Americans. (p.30)

The present system needs a fundamental overhaul. (p.34)

Greater economic parity among North America, East Asia and Europe has caused a sea change in world trade and finance. We have no choice but to move from what was formerly the hegemony of a single country to collective management by the industrial democracies. (p.36)

The Commission strongly endorses a major U.S. commitment to the successful transition of the former Soviet bloc. We have taken on such a challenge before and been the better for it. (p.33)

IV. America's Stake in Global Issues

Many measures of human impact – from water use
to the emissions of trace gases – show greater change
since 1950 than in the previous 10,000 years. (p.38)

In the war against drugs, like so much
else on our national agenda, it is time
to wage the battle at home. (p.52)

During the Cold War, we celebrated the right to leave.
Now we must promote the right to stay. (p.50)

Greater efficiency in energy use is essential
for the United States. Higher energy prices
are unavoidable. (p.44)

The worst-case scenario?
Human population could almost quadruple to 20 billion people by the year 2100. (p.40)

Many measures of human impact – from water use to the emissions of trace gases – show greater change since 1950 than in the previous 10,000 years. (p.38)

In the war against drugs, like so much else on our national agenda, it is time to wage the battle at home. (p.52)

During the Cold War, we celebrated the right to leave. *Now we must promote the right to stay.* (p.50)

Greater efficiency in energy use is essential for the United States. Higher energy prices are unavoidable. (p.44)

V. Beyond the Cold War

Now that the Cold War is over, we are free to move away from a peace that rests on a balance of terror between two armed camps toward a peace based on trust and shared interest. (p.55)

The proliferation of weapons of mass destruction is the greatest single threat to American security. (p.73)

The United States is the world's leading military power. We must keep it that way. (p.56)

We will inevitably rely more and more on collective security to cope with new military challenges – or they will not be dealt with at all. (p.65)

Now that the Cold War is over, we are free to move away from a peace that rests on a balance of terror between two armed camps toward a peace based on trust and shared interest. (p.55)

The proliferation of weapons of mass destruction is the greatest single threat to American security. (p.73)

The United States is the world's leading military power. We must keep it that way. (p.56)

We will inevitably rely more and more on collective security to cope with new military challenges – or they will not be dealt with at all. (p.65)

VI. Toward a Freer World

The end of our global rivalry with the Soviet Union sharply reduces the need to muffle our concerns about unsavory governments because of security concerns. (p.80)

Americans have two powerful allies in building democracy – the world media and the world democratic community. (p.81)

Democracy, like other elements of our foreign policy, begins at home. (p.82)

The end of our global rivalry with the Soviet Union sharply reduces the need to muffle our concerns about unsavory governments because of security concerns. (p.80)

Americans have two powerful allies in building democracy – the world media and the world democratic community. (p.81)

Democracy, like other elements of our foreign policy, begins at home. (p.82)

VII. Changing Our Ways

We are a country ill-equipped for new priorities. Our institutions creak with anachronisms. Many leaders proclaim change but act as if nothing has changed. And we are not preparing the next generation of Americans to understand, much less lead, in a transformed world. (p.85)

It will be the character and quality of people, not the adequacy of machinery, that will determine success. (p.86)

We are a country ill-equipped for new priorities. Our institutions creak with anachronisms. Many leaders proclaim change but act as if nothing has changed. And we are not preparing the next generation of Americans to understand, much less lead, in a transformed world. (p.85)

It will be the character and quality of people, not the adequacy of machinery, that will determine success. (p.86)

… An old world is collapsing and a new world arising; we have better eyes for the collapse than for the rise, for the old one is the world we know."

John Updike

I. The New Landscape

Twice before in this century the United States and our allies triumphed in a global struggle. Twice before we earned the right to be an arbiter of a postwar world. This is our third chance.

Our first chance to enact a bold new foreign policy came in 1919. Despite Woodrow Wilson's good intentions, our response was too idealistically conceived, too rigidly presented. Our goals were beyond our grasp. But when America was given a second opening after World War II, wise leaders tempered idealism with realism.

Certainly the Cold War was a time of great tension and internal dispute. There were moments when we were not true to our ideals at home or abroad. But the policies put into play starting in 1947 ultimately succeeded in their fundamental objective four decades later — the containment and defeat of Soviet Communism.

Now America once again faces a rare opportunity, an open but fleeting moment in world history. We must seize it now. This is our chance to ensure that recent enemies become future friends and that present allies do not become new antagonists. This is our chance to shape new forms of leadership before the fluid trends of the moment harden into something not to our liking. Above all, this is the time for us to change the way we think about the world and the way we conduct our affairs at home and abroad.

The world we have known for half a century is rapidly receding into history. A new world is emerging as a strange shape, unformed, yet forming fast. Familiar landmarks are changing before we can adjust our thinking.

This Commission is composed of a score of Americans with experience in domestic and foreign policy in elected and appointed public office, academia, diplomacy, journalism, the military, science, business and labor. Among us are Democrats, Republicans and independents. We set ourselves an ambitious goal: in a brief report to describe a rapidly changing world and chart a new direction for American foreign policy.

We have sought to sketch the outlines for an emerging national debate, one that should be waged beyond Washington, D.C., beyond academic cloisters — in town halls, union halls and schools across the country.

We began by examining the most important features of the new international landscape. We soon found identifying the challenges of even the immediate future a more difficult task than we anticipated. After all, not one member of this Commission foresaw that the Cold War would end the way it did in the late 1980s, that our adversary's territory would be splintered, its ideology so discredited.

Nor did we predict that stubborn regional conflicts, from Southern Asia to Central America, would have been so quickly tamed or resolved. We watch with cautious hope as apartheid is dismantled in South Africa. We are pleased that bitter adversaries in the Middle East have finally begun to talk to each other about peace.

Americans have been privileged to witness nations reborn in peace and liberty: Germany reunited, Eastern Europe liberated and Latin American juntas replaced by freely elected governments. The United Nations has begun to fulfill the vision of its founders. Revolutions in technology, transportation and communications are bettering lives and freeing minds.

And yet ours is a paradoxical victory. There has been no Victory-over-Communism Day, no confetti, no strangers kissing in the street. Indeed, it has been a long time since America has been so uneasy about itself and so uncertain of where to go next.

As Americans look abroad, our euphoria over the crumbling of the Berlin Wall has given way to the realization of how complex the challenges ahead will be. We see countries that rejected Communism now struggling to define themselves. We see ancient tribal forces and virulent nationalisms destroying societies and producing millions of refugees. Even in leading democracies – Germany, France, Italy, Canada and Japan – governments face rising levels of public distrust.

This is no less true of our own country, where our domestic progress seems arrested by political gridlock and public debt. Citizens worry that America's way of life is at the mercy of international events and foreign economic forces. After decades of global exertion, Americans now seem in the mood for retrenchment. Some politicians are listening, declaring that it's time to take care of our own.

We don't disagree. Indeed, the need for a domestic national renewal is self-evident, overwhelming and urgent. But how do we "take care of our own" in a world where it takes hours to cross the oceans, minutes to flash news or seconds to transfer wealth? The old adage is still true: domestic policy is important, but foreign policy can kill you. Today foreign policy can also raise or lower the cost of your home mortgage, create a new job or cause you to lose the one you've got.

This Commission therefore believes that our domestic renewal will require America's active engagement abroad. The affairs of the world have become too deeply integrated into the fabric of our domestic life for us simply to ignore the rest of the globe while we concentrate on our domestic priorities.

Our problems at home are serious, and our challenges abroad as daunting as they are ambiguous. But neither are insurmountable, and progress in one area is necessary to advance our objectives in the other.

America must begin the process of creating a new national consensus on foreign policy. Such a consensus is as important today as it was in 1947. Before writing this report, we held hearings, solicited views across America and conducted lengthy meetings. We have learned through our work that we still have serious differences. We agree, however, on fundamental American interests and America's role in the world.

No member of this Commission subscribes to everything in this report. But all of us share a sense of urgency sharpened by our inquiry. We confined ourselves to major issues. While we do not claim to have found all the right answers, we hope we have raised some of the right questions.

We debated the fate of NATO in the new world as well as how to block the proliferation of weapons of mass destruction. We examined issues never given prominence in U.S. foreign policy such as environmental degradation. We questioned whether regional trade arrangements are desirable extensions of a global market.

We conclude that no single doctrine like containment will serve as an organizing principle for American foreign policy. For all its success containment was narrow in purpose. While it warded off a grave threat, it often required shunting aside other goals. Efforts to halt nuclear proliferation, promote democracy, and improve the competitive position of American industries and workers, were all sacrificed or compromised at times to the overriding goal of containing Communism.

We may face new threats to our security, and we cannot be indifferent to conflict and instability in regions where we have vital national interests such as Europe, the Middle East and Northeast Asia. But we can be more selective about where and how we become engaged than during our global competition with the Soviet Union.

Most fundamentally, we are now free to move away from the armed truce of the Cold War toward a durable peace that is more than the absence of war. We are also free to press more vigorously for other basic objectives of foreign policy: prosperity at home and development abroad, the solution of ecological problems and the expansion of human rights and freedom.

This stance will require a marked change in emphasis and approach. Protecting our security and advancing our prosperity have been prime objectives since the birth of the republic. But the day is passed when we could hope to realize them unilaterally. Creating a more democratic world has long been an American ideal. Today, when we can work with an expanding community of democracies, it is an ideal both more feasible and more important. So, too, is the goal of environmental protection. Preserving a habitable planet is an urgent addition to our foreign policy agenda.

America cannot sustain an effective foreign policy unless the American people are confident that our efforts abroad serve our interests at home. This must be the bedrock of any new consensus.

America's well-being in turn depends as never before on the well-being of other countries. Growth in the markets of Europe, Japan and the developing world can create new jobs for Americans. Our environment can be harmed by coal burning in India and China or deforestation in Latin America. And as we saw in the Persian Gulf, our own security is more dependent on our ability to build collective responses to aggression.

We must also keep faith with our ideals. When brave Chinese citizens died near Tiananmen Square, they fell before a "Goddess of Democracy" that evoked the Statue of Liberty. If their faith in democracy struck some as naive, it expressed the spirit of the age and possibilities for the future.

We believe that in the new world three fundamental principles should guide America:

- First, our foreign policy must be founded on a renewal of our domestic strength; rebuilding our economic base is now our highest priority.

- Second, our national interests require continued American leadership in the world; we must not retreat into neo-isolationism or protectionism.

- Third, our leadership must be of a new kind – one that mobilizes collective action; few great goals can be reached without America, but America can no longer reach many of them alone.

The Commission advocates four broad objectives for the United States:

For a more prosperous America and a more prosperous world we must:

- Adopt an aggressive strategy for economic revival at home that favors investment in the future over consumption for the moment;

- Overhaul the international system of trade and finance, moving toward effective collective leadership by the major industrialized countries;

- Renew our commitment to help poor nations; and

- Invest in the future of former Communist countries.

For a more **livable** planet we must:

- Increase our energy efficiency by significantly raising energy prices, lifting our performance toward that of other industrialized countries;

- Give high priority to improving the environment through sustainable economic growth and ecological agreements;

- Resume decisive American leadership in world population policy;

- Develop a stronger multilateral approach toward humanitarian crises and migration; and

- Combat our drug problem where it counts – at home.

For a **safer** world we must:

- Remain the leading military power even as we significantly reduce our defense spending and overseas deployments;

- Realign NATO and CSCE to deal with the new security problems in Europe;

- Strengthen the peacekeeping capacities of the United Nations and regional organizations;

- Promote collective leadership by adding Japan and Germany as permanent members of the U.N. Security Council; and

- Strive for a less militarized world by cutting in this decade global defense expenditures to half of their 1988 peak, reducing weapons of mass destruction and halting their proliferation.

For a **freer** world we must:

- Practice at home what we preach abroad about liberty and justice; and

- Build democracies through multilateral pressures and incentives.

These goals frequently overlap and tend to reinforce one another. The advance of democracy enhances prospects for peace. The promotion of cost-effective energy efficiency helps national security, economic growth and the environment. But our goals can clash as well. Rapid democratization can produce instability. Rapid adjustment to "greener" policies can disrupt industries.

The goals we have proposed will not be easily achieved. They will require sustained, unified national effort. We will have to make hard choices. As we go forward, the United States must be unsentimental in separating the essential from the desirable.

What is required is a fusion of our values and our needs. Now that the Cold War is over, America must not revert to a cycle of expansive idealism alternating with narrow self-interest – both, at heart, forms of unilateralism. It is time to build a consensus on new priorities.

"Whatever America hopes to bring to pass in the world must first come to pass in the heart of America."

Dwight D. Eisenhower

"Whatever America hopes to bring to pass in the the world must first come to pass in the heart of America."

Dwight D. Eisenhower

II. New Priorities

The wider world is no longer an exotic realm. Ancient spice trails and caravan routes are now the subject of tedious negotiations. Foreign leaders – Deng, Walesa, Yeltsin – now seem as familiar as big city mayors.

While foreign policy has lost glamour, domestic policy has gained urgency. But the two are no longer neat and separate. Tangled strands, they stretch and intertwine across national borders.

There is, however, one constant for any policy, foreign or domestic, that aspires to be both visionary and realistic. It must favor the long term over the short term, the future over immediate gratification. In this sense our challenge abroad is akin to that at home.

For example, we should not, and need not, choose between investing in a poorly performing American educational system and a poorly performing Russian democracy. Both can be wise investments in America's future.

This Commission had neither the mandate nor the time to explore the domestic scene in depth. Yet we are convinced that Americans not only need to pay urgent attention to our problems at home, but also must agree on a vision of the future.

Our foreign policy also must enlist the support of the American people. Our international agenda should reflect our national priorities. Foreign policy must help create American jobs, protect the American environment, assure American security and reflect American values.

To advance our interests abroad we must get our own house in order. An America that lacks economic strength and social cohesion will lose respect abroad. Others will set our agenda. If our domestic problems worsen, if our international competitiveness erodes, we will lack the means, the political will and the credibility to lead. We might then be tempted to turn away from the world. Too many of us are already blaming others for problems made in America.

There is a widespread belief that the burden of protecting West Europe and East Asia has left us weaker and less competitive abroad. America certainly carried a heavy load over the last fifty years. Yet we must also look elsewhere for the sources of our current economic ills. For example, we spend 13 percent of our national income on health care, double that spent by Japan, and more than double what we now spend on defense. The American economy could get a greater boost from making health care more cost-effective than from further deep cuts in our national defense.

Increasingly we judge ourselves against other nations and find ourselves lacking. Americans are ashamed – or should be – to be nineteenth in infant mortality. We are far behind the near-perfect literacy rates of Germany and South Korea. We have become the world's largest debtor while Japan is the world's largest creditor.

There is a recognition here as well as abroad that America faces an accumulation of economic and social ills: meager savings and investment, excessive debt, a troubled public school system, an eroding infrastructure, racial tensions, crime and drugs. These deficiencies must be corrected. If not they are certain to corrode our future.

We face a serious challenge but hardly a desperate one. Our government may be broke, but our country is not poor. America remains the world's foremost economic power. But we are paying a price for evading hard choices. Our crisis is essentially political, not economic.

Victory's Dividend

The Commission urges the reduction of the federal budget deficit and the early balancing of current expenditures with current receipts. Our eventual goal should be a budget surplus. There is no painless solution to the deficit. We will need stronger discipline over spending, including limits on entitlement programs, as well as increases in taxes.

We recognize that it is hardly a great act of courage for an unelected Commission to take this stand. But we are convinced that if this nation is to move forward, our leaders will have to put the national interest ahead of their own careers. They must accept the burden of explanation that goes with their election to high office.

It has become fashionable in some circles to question the reality of the "peace dividend." Certainly, lowered defense spending is no magic solution to the deficit, but while defense cutbacks cannot do the whole job, they are real and substantial. For example, if the nation had chosen to reduce defense spending in 1991 to 3.0 percent of gross domestic product (GDP) instead of the actual 5.8 percent, some $145 billion would have been available for other purposes.

What these "other purposes" turn out to be will matter greatly. Reduction of the federal deficit as well as increases in education and other public investment are appropriate uses of money no longer needed for our security. Using defense savings simply to relieve the fiscal pressure arising from uncontrolled growth of entitlement programs is neither appropriate nor responsible.

Cutbacks in defense spending are already causing pain in many communities and specialized industries. Nevertheless, there are still too many bases in America that cannot be justified for military purposes, and too many arms programs that are not required for our security. The Commission believes that maintaining unnecessary defense expenditures in order to preserve jobs harms America's real economic and security interests.

For the most part we should rely on the market to sort out the reallocation of resources from defense industries to other needs. Yet public policy can facilitate the market process. We should encourage efforts to channel scientific and technical resources into civilian production. For the short term, an increased investment in public infrastructure – bridges, roads, airports – is a good way to employ workers and resources that would otherwise remain idle.

Richer and Poorer

Our economic problems become still more urgent when we attach human faces to them. Around the country there are signs that America's traditional economic optimism has given way to somber passivity. This change of mood reflects not only the lengthy recession but also a growing inequality of incomes and a prolonged stagnation of real wages. Although many more American households now have more than one breadwinner, median family incomes (which doubled from 1947 through 1973) are little higher today than they were eighteen years ago. At the upper end of the income scale, however, family incomes have risen nearly 25 percent. These widening disparities exacerbate America's social tensions.

These trends are associated in part with the increased involvement of the United States in a global economy. More and more, low-skilled but well-paid workers in industrial countries are competing with similarly skilled but lower-wage workers in developing countries. At the same time the best educated and trained workers in the industrial countries have become even more valuable in a global marketplace. The irony is that while expanded trade has raised productivity everywhere, income earners have not benefited equally.

This Commission believes it would be folly to try to withdraw from international competition in an effort to recapture an earlier era when we enjoyed large numbers of relatively high-paid, low-skill jobs. Although some Americans would gain, many more would lose.

The United States has no alternative to active participation in the worldwide economy. Expanding American exports is critical to future growth and the creation of new jobs. We need to reinforce public and private efforts to enhance our international competitiveness.

In the meantime we cannot allow the living standards of some working Americans to continue to drift downward. We must take seriously our public responsibility to design and finance effective programs of readjustment assistance for displaced workers. We should foster retraining as well as job search and relocation. There is still much we have to learn about the domestic effects of a globalized economy. But we cannot wait to begin to deal with their consequences.

Over the long term well-paid jobs will require well-educated workers. Nothing is more important to this country's future than revitalizing public education.

Peace at Home

Thomas Jefferson admonished us to make America "a standing monument and example for the aim and imitation of other countries." To this day our influence in the world has stemmed not only from our economic and military muscle, but also from the force of our ideals and example. But television can undermine America's prestige and moral authority almost as well as it can expose a foreign tyrant. A videotaped police beating and bloody riots in Los Angeles were transformed by television into events of world significance. These same images were a graphic reminder to all Americans that racism, chronic poverty and crime remain disturbing features of our society.

America today is struggling to reconcile the tensions between the need for national unity and the right of individuals and groups to be different. Many Americans are insisting not only on preserving their cultural identity, a goal that is wholly desirable, but also on something akin to cultural and political separatism. As Arthur Schlesinger, Jr., has written: "Instead of a nation composed of individuals making their own free choices, America increasingly sees itself as composed of groups more or less indelible in their ethnic character. . . .Will the center hold?"

This Commission believes that, for all its faults, America has confronted this dilemma better than any other multiethnic nation. Consider the vast numbers who still seek to come to these shores from the highlands of Laos and Guatemala, from the cities of Nigeria and India. Though all come seeking opportunity, they want more than a job. They want to be Americans.

A prominent journalist recently reminded us that "The notion of a vast foreign public cackling in glee at American discomfort dies hard. I think most of the world is almost desperately eager to see the United States succeed." For 200 years America has been a model of a successful representative republic. From 1863 on – and especially since 1964 – the American model has been improved. The American spirit continues to have resonance around the globe.

Our multiethnic society also gives Americans the skills needed in a new world: respecting differences while advancing common goals, mobilizing coalitions and making compromises.

We must not deceive ourselves that our multiethnic heritage, unique as it is, prepares us to understand feuds that predate our republic. Still, if we can bring together the sons and daughters of Europe, Asia, Africa and Latin America in one land, we offer a better vision to Armenian and Turk, Romanian and Hungarian, Arab and Israeli.

New Leadership for a New World

"In the years before 1914 America was a great power. . . . In the years to come it will still be the only nation able to beat back aggression, as it has just done in the Gulf. It will neither want nor be able to do that alone; nor could America before 1914. But it will be unique in the way in which it can project power to help its allies. Like America before 1914 it will be a country with which everyone wants to be friends."

The Economist

America can end the century much as we began it – a great power regarded widely as an honest broker. Yet our world is transformed.

Simply put, the First World has been radically altered. The Second and Third Worlds no longer exist.

One-quarter of humanity still lives under the red banner in China, North Korea, Vietnam and Cuba. But Communism is spent as a world force. The so-called Second World of Communism has vanished in Europe and the former Soviet Union. Within that vast zone, fragile and dissimilar nations are coalescing around old Slavic, Turkic and other roots.

As for the Third World, that expression no longer describes anything. This lumping together of varied societies has long since broken up into an archipelago, some islands of relative prosperity and democracy, others of crushing poverty and cruel dictatorship. An underclass of nations has emerged.

Meanwhile, in the First World the phoenix-like rise of Europe and Japan has fulfilled the vision of one of America's most cherished foreign policy goals. The years just after World War II left America supreme and unchallenged throughout most of the world. Through our postwar policies we helped create a triad of wealthy and successful democracies. America today is no longer dominant but it remains first among equals. The relative power of other nations is far greater than before.

So, count among the many ironies of the Cold War that the victor emerged with less power, not more. This shift from dominance to preeminence means we must fundamentally change both the substance and style of our international leadership. We must respect the new boundaries of America's strength and stamina.

America must recognize that now other nations seek greater voices, not just greater burdens. We need to act more as catalyst than as commander, resorting more often to persuasion and compromise than to fiat and rigid blueprint.

But we must also recognize that without our measured leadership, the prospects for a safer, richer, cleaner, freer world would fade. So would America's future. No longer an overwhelming leader in all categories of power, America is still the only country strong in each – military, political, economic, technological, cultural and demographic. We are the only major nation with a postwar tradition of taking the risks necessary to be a world leader. We have closer relations with the other major powers than they have with one another. And we are still the only nation whose leadership most other nations are willing to follow.

The United States must reserve the option of independent action. If, for example, the international community fails to act to counter threats to our national security, we will need to move on our own.

But clear trends more and more beckon us toward collective approaches: the diffusion of power, stronger friends to carry greater responsibilities, the global nature of new problems, the growing effectiveness of multilateral institutions. Our central approach in foreign policy should be to seek, build and lead coalitions of nations to advance our common interests in security, prosperity, the environment and the expansion of the democratic community.

This emphasis on collective leadership can no longer be merely a facade or afterthought. In the new world acting jointly with others will often be the only way we can extend our influence and advance our goals.

We can exercise such leadership in many ways. None is more crucial than working with our major democratic partners in the Group of Seven (G-7). We must also be ready to manage *ad hoc* coalitions with other nations as we did during the Gulf War. We need to strengthen our role in multilateral institutions like the United Nations. As we do so, we must never lose sight of the bottom line: multilateralism must serve American interests. It is not an end in itself.

Collective action will also have costs. Working with others can be cumbersome and demanding. It is terribly difficult to build consensus and forge a common agenda among sovereign countries when there are differences in self-interest. The task is still more arduous with democracies whose governments – like ours – are accountable to shifting public opinion. Yet, if we are not prepared to address the interests and concerns of others, they will move without us and our influence will be eroded. The June 1992 Rio Conference on Environment and Development demonstrated many of these difficulties.

If we are to succeed with a new kind of leadership, we will sometimes have to yield a measure of the autonomy we have guarded so zealously during most of our history. It is not enough for the United States to say that we will pursue common goals on our own. We must be genuinely prepared to meet our obligations under multilateral agreements.

The challenges of collective leadership will be especially demanding in the management of our relations with the other major powers. With the end of the Cold War, the security concerns of the European and Japanese have diminished. They feel freer to pursue their own agendas and are less willing to follow an American lead. These countries are our major economic competitors. Yet without their collaboration, few of our own goals can be achieved.

America will vigorously pursue its self-interest. But in doing so, Americans will need to change the way we think about the world and our role in it. Increasingly joint action will be the most effective way to promote our interests. We will not always get all that we want. Some domestic groups will be hurt or offended and U.S. politics will become roiled. We will require firm leadership in the White House and the Congress, an informed media and an engaged public.

The World Economy

Although America continues to be the most powerful nation in the world, we no longer have the ability to overwhelm every problem with resources. We can still afford to do anything. But we can no longer afford to do everything.

Some mourn the loss of the days when America produced half of the world's wealth. It would be misleading, however, to judge America today by the unique years just after World War II. Our share of global output has returned to the level of the 1930s, close to a quarter, still large enough to be the hub of the world economy.

But we do see cause for alarm in our domestic condition. America's savings and investment rates, compared to those of our competitors, are abysmal. For the past decade we have lagged behind our major trading partners in improving our productivity; our standard of living has risen very slowly; and we have lost our edge in many industries.

The globalization of production and capital markets has greatly reduced America's economic autonomy, along with that of all other nations. A so-called American-made car is now composed of parts from around the world, as multinational as the American workforce is multiethnic. Our workers, consumers and businesses stand to gain much from free trade and lose much from trade wars.

Meanwhile, the gap between the developed and the newly industrializing countries narrows, while underclass nations fall further and further behind. The 1980s were particularly bad for non-Asian developing countries. But even here, there are some bright spots. For example, Mexico, long one of the most statist economies and severely declining in the 1980s, is privatizing whole industries and opening to the world. Even in the midst of an international recession Mexico is enjoying economic growth.

The Health of the Planet

When the Cold War began, the world was populated by about 2.5 billion people. Today, more than twice as many inhabit the earth. U.N. population projections for the year 2025 range from 7.6 billion to 9.4 billion. Some estimates foresee populations of almost 20 billion by the end of the next century.

As world population increases geometrically, new concerns, like environmental degradation and vast migration flows, will loom ever larger on foreign policy agendas.

While the populations of high-fertility poor nations explode, the most prosperous industrialized nations have low fertility and stable populations. In the past, only when nations reached a critical threshold of prosperity have they begun to alleviate many environmental and demographic pressures. Today, however, if poorer countries wait to tackle these problems, they will never achieve even a modest level of economic success.

We have heard previous warnings about environmental and demographic devastation. If we have become complacent about these problems, perhaps it is because we became inured long ago by alarmist rhetoric. But while projections vary, the global challenges are serious – and increasing.

We also face a growing complex of humanitarian crises. During the past forty years great strides have been made in our capacity to control disease, diminish suffering and extend life. But progress in health has been uneven. Hunger and famine still reign over much of the earth. More than 500 million people eat fewer calories daily than are necessary for an active life – or life itself. Even where food is available, clean water often is not. Every day 40,000 children are lost to illness and malnutrition. Millions continue to suffer and die from diseases that can be prevented and treated.

The explosive increase in the flows of people, goods and ideas around the globe has created new health issues. It has both advanced health education and treatment and contributed to the spread of disease – be it AIDS, cholera or dengue hemorrhagic fever. Diseases that in earlier times might have remained local curses now have global range. In an increasingly open world, advancing world health not only helps others but also protects the health of Americans.

AIDS is the most dramatic example of growing global interdependence in health. One million Americans are estimated to be infected with human immunodeficiency virus (HIV), which causes AIDS. Around the world at least 12-14 million people are HIV positive. During the next decade the HIV virus is likely to spread into most communities. There is still neither vaccine nor cure. Borders cannot protect against it. It is a global problem. It requires a global approach.

Greater Security, Less Self-Reliance

The collapse of the Soviet Union has left the United States the only power with worldwide reach. And the defeat of the Iraqi force in Kuwait demonstrated that a new generation of American weapons can dominate the conventional battlefield.

But substantial threats persist. At least one state, Russia, will still have the ability to destroy America with its nuclear forces, even after the deep cuts agreed to in June 1992 for the next decade. And most ominously, the technology to make and deliver weapons of mass destruction is proliferating among some of the least savory regimes on earth. Some of these nations, from North Korea to Libya to Iran, remain hostile to the United States.

Acting alone the United States lacks the resources to secure stability and democracy in the new world. Despite our military power America is in no position unilaterally to cause states to demilitarize peacefully, to curb nuclear proliferation or contain ethnic explosions. It is becoming more difficult to translate military dominance into political influence.

Fortunately the end of the Cold War has removed major roadblocks to international cooperation. In particular, the superpower deadlock that paralyzed the United Nations has been broken. The organization has been freed to take vigorous action unthinkable just a few years ago – mediation, peacemaking and peacekeeping.

The Flowering of Freedom

For the first time in history, a majority of countries practice some form of government that can be called democratic. But when we speak of the flowering of freedom, the metaphor could be more accurate than we intended – new democracies can be fragile and tragically short-lived.

The ending of a forty-year stalemate has loosened restraints on violence between and within nations. For every Namibia there is a Somalia, for every Hungary a Yugoslavia. Peoples are being pushed together by the need to cooperate, while being pulled apart by ethnic antagonism. The countries that have arisen out of the demise of the Soviet Union face a deeply uncertain future. Democracy and nationalism will not always be allies.

The cry for self-determination is heard throughout the world. We must not assume that it is always a call for democracy. In fact it is sometimes an ethnic ambition that narrows human rights rather than expands them. In recent years people power has razed walls, toppled governments and pulverized ideologies. But people power has also destroyed whole villages and driven millions of innocents into the mountains or onto the high seas.

The world has also been irrevocably transformed by the information revolution. Fax machines, telephones and television punched holes through the Iron Curtain. Tyrants can no longer insulate their people from the outside world nor shield themselves from scrutiny. Chinese demonstrators kindled the resistance of East Germans, who inspired the Czechs, who emboldened the Romanians – a chain reaction of human courage that swept from Asia to the heart of Europe, all the way back to Mongolia.

In the following chapters, we stress the themes of domestic renewal and collective leadership. By changing our ways, America can flourish in this new era while staying true to our interests and our ideals.

"Prosperity has no fixed limits. It is not a finite substance to be diminished by division. On the contrary, the more of it that other nations enjoy, the more each nation will have for itself."

Henry Morgenthau
Bretton Woods
April 1944

"Prosperity has no fixed limits. It is not a finite substance to be diminished by division. On the contrary, the more of it that other nations enjoy, the more each nation will have for itself."

III. The Challenges of a World Economy

The American Economic Position

Through much of the Cold War, the United States enjoyed growing prosperity despite a heavy burden of military spending. We were not only the leader of the Western alliance, but also the architect and manager of an international economic system that generated growth among ally and recent enemy alike. The widening circle of world prosperity helped win the Cold War and contributed to our own well-being.

One consequence of the success of our policies is that while the United States remains the largest economy in the world, it is no longer the dominant one. Three economic superpowers, both competing and cooperating, have replaced the bipolar world. In terms of comparative purchasing power – an appropriate gauge of relative standards of living – the U.S. position has changed little since 1960 relative to the twelve current members of the European Community (EC). Compared to Japan, however, U.S. GDP has gone from six and a half times as large to only two and a half times as large. When national output is compared using current exchange rates – appropriate for assessing strength in international markets – the EC's production is larger than that of the United States. Moreover, the EC is far closer to a unified economy today than it was in 1960 and increasingly acts as a single player on the world economic stage (Table 1).

Productivity is another good measure of the dramatic change in the U.S. position. Real output per capita in 1960 in Japan and the EC-12 was approximately 30 percent as great as in the United States. In 1990 Japan's productivity had reached more than 80 percent of ours, and that of the EC-12 about 65 percent.

Over decades this kind of economic convergence is natural, even desirable. The normal processes of trade, investment and competition may steadily reduce a leading economy's technological and productivity advantages, but all parties benefit. Such natural convergence explains much of the narrowing gap between the United States and other industrial nations during the postwar period. By itself it will not relegate the United States to second-class status.

Table 1: Real Gross Domestic Product

Based on Purchasing Power Parity

		Total			Per Capita		
		1960	**1980**	**1990**	**1960**	**1980**	**1990**
	U.S.	100.0	100.0	100.0	100.0	100.0	100.0
	EC-12	81.4	91.8	85.8	29.4	65.9	66.3
	Japan	15.3	34.2	39.0	29.0	67.6	80.7

Based on Market Exchange Rates

		Total			Per Capita		
	U.S.	100.0	100.0	100.0	100.0	100.0	100.0
	EC-12	57.2	116.4	109.7	37.0	83.5	84.1
	Japan	8.7	39.5	52.5	16.6	77.0	106.7

Source:
The EC Annual Economic Report, 1990-91

Recent U.S. economic performance, however, has allowed other nations to catch up much faster than any natural economic process would warrant. Our savings and investment rates are strikingly low compared with those of other major industrial nations. The Japanese, with an economy 60 percent the size of ours, invest more than we do. Our productivity gains have lagged well behind those in other countries. We have augmented domestic savings and financed growth by running large external payments deficits – $1 trillion over the last ten years.

The Commission believes that America's first foreign policy priority is to strengthen our domestic economic performance. Unless we do so, our economy will deteriorate to the point where our position in world affairs will be decisively weakened by the turn of the century. Such a development would have profound consequences for global stability and our own security.

America must not become a second-class economic power. In the aftermath of the Cold War we are starting to divert some of the enormous resources required to wage a global military rivalry to peaceful economic and social purposes at home. If we can also reform our economic policies, U.S. dynamism will be restored. But sustained improvements demand a decisive change of course.

There are those who view the EC and especially Japan as major threats. They suggest that economic rivalry might spill over into political and even military dimensions. Japan is a focus of much of this concern because of the substantial differences between its economy and society and our own – the "lack of a level playing field."

Certainly competition among the different types of market economies will be an important feature of the international scene in the years ahead. Further American economic decline could also trigger mercantilist and protectionist policies in the United States. Turning inward would be all the more likely if Japan or the EC engages in "unfair" practices that are seen to be important sources of that decline.

We view these issues as extremely serious. This is why we place such priority on restoring American competitiveness. This is also why we attach such importance to building collective leadership of the world economy by the United States, Japan and a uniting Europe.

However, the Commission views Japan and the EC more as a challenge than as a threat. They are democracies that practice market economics, if somewhat different brands than ours. We have been firm allies for more than four decades. We have deeply ingrained habits of working together on economic as well as security issues. Because of the extensive market interpenetration of the three, any serious disruption of our economic relations would impose enormous costs on all.

Moreover, our chief competitors face substantial uncertainties of their own, giving us breathing space to address our domestic problems. Powerful new forces are reshaping the European scene: German unification, political change and economic reform in Eastern Europe and the former Soviet Union and the complicated processes of deepening and broadening the EC. Serious budgetary, social and political strains are growing in a graying Europe committed to a highly developed social market but subjected to increasingly intense international competition.

For Japan uncertainty arises from different sources. The pricking of the real estate bubble and the collapse of equity values remind us of the linkage between the real economy and financial markets – a linkage that may prove to be difficult to repair. An aging labor force and growing labor shortages complicate Japan's prospects. Moreover, many Japanese are coming to realize that private consumption is not a necessary evil but a natural outcome of economic activity. While a new era of leisure and self-indulgence is far from at hand, Japan is becoming more consumer oriented.

In any case, neither the United States, the EC nor Japan is able to go it alone. We share a common stake in an expanding global economy and improved international arrangements.

A Global Economy Takes Shape

American leadership after World War II was instrumental in establishing a liberal system of international trade and finance, including the World Bank, the International Monetary Fund (IMF), the General Agreement on Tariffs and Trade (GATT) and other multinational institutions. This system, combined with dramatic decreases in the costs of transportation and communication, led to the emergence of a global economy far freer and more integrated than the restricted and compartmentalized one of the early postwar period. Over the last thirty years world trade has more than tripled.

International trade is now central to all successful economies including our own. It increasingly involves services as well as goods. Trade in manufactures is based on many factors other than natural comparative advantage. All major economies, and many minor ones, participate in a world financial market in which capital no longer "flows." It is transmitted at the speed of light.

The features of this new global economy are still evolving. They include an ever greater reliance on telecommunications; interaction between technology, production and services; and the establishment of modern industrial production in many different countries. Assembly and manufacturing operations are breaking away from national moorings everywhere, not just in America. With the proliferation of transnational corporate alliances, multinationals operate across borders at all stages of production. This underscores the need to maintain an edge in the development and application of new technologies.

In this new era, the United States is no longer a world unto itself, a continental economy rich in natural resources looking primarily inward. The character of the American economy changed in a single decade. Trade doubled as a percent of U.S. gross national product, from 12.7 percent in 1970 to 25 percent in 1980, and is still at that level, similar to its share in the EC and Japan.

One result of this globalization is that the economies of the EC and the United States are not only converging in size, they are growing to resemble each other. Europe's internal barriers to trade are falling while America's involvement in the global economy has risen. Japan, too, is slowly becoming more like Europe and the United States as its imports grow and its companies invest around the world.

The world economy is not only globalizing, it is regionalizing as well. Three regions dominate world trade – Western Europe, North America and East Asia. Taken together trade within these regions now accounts for almost half of world commerce. Trade among the three regions is growing even more rapidly (Table 2).

Table 2: The Tripolarization of World Trade

(Percentage of World Imports of Goods)

		1980	1990	
I.	**Within the Three Poles**			
	OECD Europe	28.0	33.2	
	North America[1]	5.9	6.5	Sources: International Monetary Fund, Bureau of Statistics, *Direction of Trade Statistic Yearbook*, 1981 and 1991 (Washington, D.C.); Republic of China, Ministry of Finance, Department of Statistics, *Preliminary Statistics on Exports and Imports*, Taiwan area, December 1980 and 1990 (Taipei).
	East Asia[2]	6.1	9.5	
	Subtotal (within)	40.0	49.2	
II.	**Among the Three Poles**			
	Europe-North America	7.7	8.0	Taken from: Ernest Preeg, *The U.S. Leadership Role in World Trade: Past, Present and Future* (Washington, D.C.: Center for Strategic and International Studies, 1991).
	East Asia-North America	7.1	10.5	
	Europe-East Asia	4.6	8.8	
	Subtotal (among)	19.4	27.3	[1] U.S., Canada, Mexico.
III.	**All Other**	40.6	23.5	[2] Japan, South Korea, China, Taiwan, Hong Kong, ASEAN.

Sustaining the Liberal Multilateral System

The importance of the world economy to the United States has been especially evident over the last several years. Foreign trade has been the most dynamic sector of the American economy. The improvement in the U.S. current account from 1987 to this spring accounted for some $120 billion in additional expenditures for our economy. U.S. merchandise exports now support, directly and indirectly, some 7.2 million jobs. In fact virtually all of the job growth in the manufacturing sector since 1984 has been accounted for by exports. Exports of services support nearly as many jobs as exports of manufactures.

Unfortunately, the outlook for world economic growth – and the continued rapid growth of American exports – over the next few years is clouded. The United States was the world's locomotive through much of the 1980s, then Germany and Japan took over. But today there is no locomotive, no large country that is growing and willing to accept a large increase in its imports and a sizeable deterioration in its trade balance. And policy coordination among the major countries is so ineffectual that it offers little promise of concerted action that might soon stimulate world growth.

The rapid pace of change in the global economy threatens to overwhelm existing multilateral arrangements. Leadership is urgently needed and can no longer be provided by a single power, not even the United States. But multilateral leadership has not yet developed to the point where it can take over the postwar role played by the United States. In the meantime the globalizing world economy is placing new strains on the GATT and revealing institutional and conceptual weaknesses in current systems of trade and finance.

The Commission believes that an effective liberal multilateral system of trade and finance remains essential to American prosperity. We cannot stand on the sidelines. We have a vital economic interest in the rules of the international game. The United States should press other major countries to join us in revitalizing the system.

World Trade as a World Challenge

The Commission strongly endorses the maintenance of a multilateral U.S. trade policy centered on the GATT. But we also believe that the GATT must be strengthened and reformed if it is to meet the needs of the next decade.

A successful conclusion to the Uruguay Round of trade negotiations is long overdue and urgently needed. The consequences of failure, or even of significant further delay, would be painful for the United States and most other countries.

Of course, concluding the Uruguay Round will not bring multilateral rules fully in line with the changes in the international economy. But if concluded roughly on the basis of the draft agreements under discussion in early 1992, the Round would mark a major step in this direction. It would open markets for U.S. exports in sectors where we are most competitive. A successful Round would extend GATT supervision to agriculture, textiles, services and intellectual property. It would advance the integration of developing countries into the world trading system. GATT would be in a much stronger position to resolve disputes and enforce its rulings.

Important new issues regarding financial services, foreign direct investment, public procurement, technical standards and tax policies are already on the post-Uruguay Round GATT agenda. Growing conflicts between trade and environmental concerns, and between trade and competition policies, are becoming the subjects of heated debates and need early attention. So does another important issue – workers' rights. Were the Uruguay Round to fail or be further postponed, such issues would not politely await the fullness of time for their resolution. Countries would seek to deal with them through bilateral and regional deals, leading to further conflict.

Some maintain that the weakening of the GATT system would be no great loss. They believe the principles of non-discrimination and national treatment that underlie GATT negotiations are outdated. They argue that GATT is unable to cope with intrusive new trade issues that until recently were considered solely matters of domestic policy. It is claimed that cumbersome global negotiations on such matters cannot be expected to succeed and that regional negotiations offer more promise. "Reciprocity" rather than non-discrimination would be the outcome. "Free riders" would not be able to take advantage of the system.

The Commission does not share this view. We support the GATT because it opens markets for our exports and provides a mechanism for resolving trade disputes, including our own. In addition GATT offers the best way of giving all countries, including developing ones, a stake in the system. Sweetheart deals among the few are no substitute for a world trade system open to all.

The Commission found the question of regional trade groupings particularly complex. We concluded that such agreements are not necessarily inconsistent with our interest in a strong global trading system.

Regional arrangements may be helpful in promoting the integration of national markets. One powerful motive for their establishment is the need to catch up with new problems and opportunities generated by the expansion of intra-regional trade and investment. Regional arrangements are sometimes better suited than multilateral negotiations for harmonizing the varied administrative and regulatory practices across national markets, as the agreements to create a single, unified market in Europe (EC-92) and the U.S.-Canada Free Trade Agreement (FTA) demonstrate.

But it is essential that regional arrangements develop within the discipline of a strong GATT system. As trade barriers are lowered within a region, there must be no new barriers to goods and services imported from outside that region. Thus, the rise of regionalism is another strong reason to complete the Uruguay Round and address new trade issues promptly.

The FTA seems a success, notwithstanding the political controversy it has aroused in our recession-stricken neighbor. The Commission supports, in principle, revision of the agreement to include Mexico in a North American FTA. The radical change in Mexican economic policies under the government of Mexican President Carlos Salinas de Gortari has opened up the prospect of a prospering Mexico. In addition to trade, both countries must address environmental protection and the treatment of labor, as well as effective worker adjustment provisions. Too often in the past, the U.S. government has paid only lip service to worker retraining. Over time a North American Free Trade Agreement (NAFTA) can be expected to generate many more American jobs through additional exports than would be lost to additional imports. It could also help U.S. corporations become more competitive globally through coproduction strategies.

NAFTA should also bring stronger economic growth to Mexico and over time help reduce the flow of immigrants to the United States. Mexican economic success will also sustain further progress toward democratic pluralism.

What happens next is less clear. The Commission supports further carefully negotiated accessions to NAFTA by other countries in the hemisphere. The eventual goal of a hemispheric free trade zone may have appeal, but we do not believe it could ever be an acceptable alternative for the United States to an open global trading regime.

The United States does have a powerful interest in supporting economic reform in Latin America and the Caribbean. There is clear potential for major growth in our trade and investment in the region. The Commission believes the Enterprise for the Americas Initiative is an important new element in our approach to the region. We can further support the movement of Latin American and Caribbean governments toward market-oriented economic policies by providing measured debt relief and by funding a new Inter-American Development Bank facility to spur private investment.

The further integration of the European Community should be welcomed by the United States, provided that it continues to occur within GATT guidelines. At the same time the EC must demonstrate a willingness to accept its multilateral responsibilities and negotiate in areas where others believe their interests are involved. Geography and history alone make a compelling case for European economic unity. Deep, irreversible integration of national economies is also the best guarantee of political stability in Western Europe. A strong EC can also be central to the economic transformation of Eastern Europe and the former Soviet Union.

A Pacific Basin trade arrangement, including both Japan and the United States, might at some point be a goal worth pursuing. For the immediate future, however, strengthening the multilateral system is a higher priority. The Asian Pacific Economic Council (APEC), which includes the United States and Canada, is the most promising vehicle for closer economic cooperation within Asia and across the Pacific. But APEC must be strengthened and given a more substantial mandate. It could, for example, supplement GATT efforts to monitor the trade policies of its members and coordinate positions on multilateral trade issues. It could also establish mileposts for reducing trade and investment barriers within the region. It might also be opened to others in this hemisphere, such as Mexico.

U.S.-Japanese trade disputes are a common feature of the "bilateral track" of trade policy that has become so prominent in recent years. Many nations today are negotiating their trade problems on a bilateral basis outside GATT. Not surprisingly the overall impact has been strongly protectionist. The United States has not been alone in raising import barriers through such means. Twenty of the twenty-four countries in the OECD have done the same over the past decade.

The GATT's dispute settlement process has been improved since 1988, but major problems remain. Indeed, as the Uruguay Round drags on and new trade issues stack up, GATT rules are gradually becoming less and less relevant to real world trade complaints and grievances. In these circumstances, unilateral trade actions (such as those provided for under Section 301 of the Trade Act of 1988) can contribute to liberalizing world trade in the short run by helping to open other markets. But continuing to negotiate extensive bilateral arrangements outside of GATT may also undermine the multilateral system and lead to a more contentious trade environment.

The stakes of trade negotiations have been raised by the growing salience of technology. It is apparent that early government support can be critical in some strategic industries where economies of scale are critical and where "learning by doing" is essential in developing a particular technology. Programs to encourage research and development

---

Statement by Mr. Donahue

This section paints an idealized version of a non-existent free trade world, exaggerates our economy's dependence on expanding exports, pretends that the "successful" conclusion of the Uruguay Round and the NAFTA negotiations will add many more jobs than will be lost and notes innocently that a hemispheric free trade zone seems appealing.

This section fails to note the continuing restrictions on trade imposed by our "trading partners" and accepts the total deregulation of trade, eliminating any role for government. The resulting trade would be driven only by multinational corporations' decisions on where goods are produced and under what conditions, in a grossly imperfect market, without regard to national economic effects.

A hemispheric free trade zone that ignores the questions of external tariffs, fiscal and monetary policies, conditions of work and compensation, variances in standards of living of a magnitude of ten to one, occupational safety and health, child labor and environmental issues – to name just a few – is a "zone" in which the standard of living will fall to that of the lowest common denominator.

The creation of opportunities for multinational corporations to exploit cheap labor does nothing for workers. So-called "co-production strategies" encourage companies to move jobs out of the U.S. rather than to seek productivity improvements in the U.S. based on new investments in capital equipment and workers. The loss of 1.1 million U.S. jobs in manufacturing in the period 1984 to 1992 demonstrates the effects of such decisions.

Mexico needs and deserves U.S. support in its development efforts – debt forgiveness, interest payment relief, developmental assistance and programs of economic cooperation – designed to improve the conditions of life of the people of Mexico. A trade policy designed to increase the opportunities of U.S.-based multinational corporations to invest there and to repatriate profits, while creating low-wage jobs, is the wrong approach.

(R&D) and support new technologies exist in many countries. The Commission believes that the United States should consider such programs as an element of an overall competitiveness strategy.

It will be difficult to accommodate national programs to develop new technologies within an open multilateral system. Multilateral rules providing for more transparent R&D subsidies and government procurement policies could help defuse the problem. Domestic efforts to assist key industries can be compatible with a liberal multilateral trading system, as long as the support is open to international review and adjustment.

Money Matters

If the system of international trade has reached a critical juncture, the international monetary system seems to have reached an impasse. The collapse of fixed exchange rates in 1971-73 has not led to durable international understandings regarding exchange rates, international liquidity, responsibilities of debtor and creditor nations or even policy cooperation to alleviate recession. Present arrangements have grown in the absence of agreement on something more coherent.

In Europe the inflationary strains of German unification have led to the imposition of higher interest rates by the Bundesbank – a policy that reflects German domestic conditions but is inconsistent with the needs of other economies hit hard by recession. As a result, the Exchange Rate Mechanism of the European Monetary System has become less a guarantor of prudent domestic policies and more a deflationary straitjacket on the European economy. This situation could continue as the EC progresses towards monetary union. On the broader international scene a persistently weaker yen than the United States or Europe believes appropriate augurs poorly for near-term trade relations.

When the world emerges from recession and the pace of economic activity picks up, there is danger of a global capital shortage and even higher real interest rates. This would be painful for the United States, given our large budget deficit and huge public and private debt. It would be even more painful for developing countries, particularly if world savings were again channeled to industrial countries to sustain private consumption and public sector deficits.

On the brighter side the substantial progress of the U.S. and some other major countries in reducing inflation and dampening inflationary expectations is a major achievement. This success creates an important opportunity for cooperative policies among major industrial countries to encourage vigorous global growth.

Unfortunately present international monetary arrangements do not easily lend themselves to the development of a growth initiative. The IMF today plays only a limited role on global financial issues. The G-7, with an ever-changing list of heads of state and senior officials and virtually no institutional memory, has intermittently and ineffectively attempted international financial coordination.

We must do better. The G-7 should be strengthened so that it can develop a coherent approach to international monetary cooperation, the management of exchange rates and the coordination of domestic economic policies. Over time the G-7 might be gradually converted to a more efficient G-3, composed of the EC, the United States and Japan. However it evolves, the G-7 will continue to find itself drawn into a wider range of issues, including trade strategy and assistance to developing countries, Eastern Europe and the former Soviet Union.

Developing Nations in a Global Economy

The United States will be a major beneficiary as growth spreads among developing countries. We are in an especially strong competitive position to meet their needs for capital goods and equipment. In 1991, for example, U.S. exports to developing countries rose to almost $150 billion, roughly 35 percent of total U.S. exports.

The concept of a "Third World" is no longer useful or accurate. The label of "developing nations" is only a little more precise, for it now includes an increasing number of so-called newly industrializing countries (NICs), a variety of almost-NICs in Latin America and Asia, oil exporters of varying degrees of wealth and development, a worrisome number of countries still mired in stagnation and poverty, former Communist countries and a few remaining Communist states.

NICs and potential NICs are becoming more prominent in world trade and as sites for foreign investment. Many developing countries are experiencing greater growth as they adopt effective market-driven strategies.

But while some countries are graduating to industrial status, most are not. Except for East Asia per-capita income growth has been greater in high-income countries than in developing countries, particularly in the 1980s (Table 3). The stagnation of many developing economies in the 1980s was a partial result of the oil price shocks of 1973 and 1979-81 and the explosion of international debt.

**Table 3: Annual Percentage Growth Rates in Per Capita Income
in High-Income and Developing Countries**

	1960-70	1970-80	1980-90
High-Income Countries	4.1	2.4	2.4
Developing Countries	3.3	3.0	1.2
(East Asia alone)	(3.6)	(4.6)	(6.3)

Source:
World Bank *World Development
Report*, 1992.

Between 1982, when the debt crisis first hit, and 1987, net resource flows (loans, grants and foreign direct investment) to developing countries fell by half. In many heavily indebted countries, the servicing of past loans still exceeds new revenues. For developing countries as a group, net transfers are in fact negative. For some African countries, debt write-offs have become unavoidable.

Latin American states with sound domestic policies (like Chile and Mexico) have been able to negotiate reductions in their external debt and regain access to commercial sources of external finance. Others may be able to do so soon, as more countries learn to attract back capital driven off by economic instability and shortsighted policies.

Nonetheless, while Mexico, Korea and a few others will be able to attract net capital from abroad, most developing countries in the 1990s will have to finance their domestic investment requirements largely from their own resources. Collectively, they will still be providing capital to the rest of the world by running a trade surplus. Concessional aid for the world's poorer countries will remain extremely tight, partly because of new requirements of the states of Eastern Europe and the former Soviet Union.

Still, for those developing nations whose governments adopt and stick to sound market-oriented domestic policies, the next decade could be a time of remarkable progress. But such progress will require a more favorable international environment than present arrangements are likely to produce, including lower real interest rates, open markets and greater access to technology. If these trends converge, we could see the experience of the Asian "tigers" repeated elsewhere.

Over the long term the population of industrial countries will continue to shrink relative to world population. In 1980 one of every four people lived in today's high-income industrial nations. At the turn of the century, U.N. projections show that a little more than one in five will live in a high-income country; by 2025, fewer than one in six will, unless a number of low-income countries begin to grow much more rapidly. Because the population of today's industrial nations is aging much faster than that of developing countries, their share of the world's work force is declining even faster; by 2025, only one in eight workers in the world will live in one of today's high-income countries.

It does not take much imagination to conclude that our prosperity, environmental conditions and security will be affected by the economic and social development of these low- and medium-income countries. The next two decades are critical for industrial countries to create conditions for global economic expansion and social development. After that, the rising proportion of the elderly in the populations of the United States and other industrial countries may limit our ability to do so.

Indeed, in the U.S. demographic changes are likely to exacerbate intergenerational strains, as we are witnessing in the debate over entitlements. Such strains can be considerably eased if in the interim we have made profitable investments in prospering developing countries.

Developing countries are also central to resolving global issues of the environment, energy, food, health, population growth, drug trafficking, refugees and illegal immigration. These issues, discussed later in more detail, all require early attention and resources in order to forestall much heavier costs.

U.S. Budget

FY 1993 (Estimated)

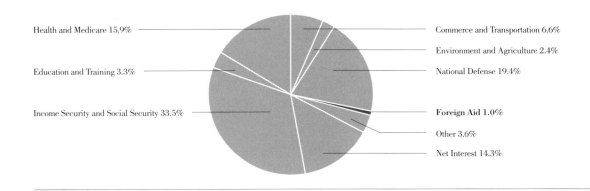

Health and Medicare 15.9%

Education and Training 3.3%

Income Security and Social Security 33.5%

Commerce and Transportation 6.6%

Environment and Agriculture 2.4%

National Defense 19.4%

Foreign Aid 1.0%

Other 3.6%

Net Interest 14.3%

Source:
Budget of the United States
Government, FY93.

Finally, practical considerations aside, we still have a moral interest in reducing global poverty. Hundreds of millions of people are born each year into a world of deprivation and desperation unimaginable to most Americans. Trade and private investment cannot do the whole job. Vigorous leadership will be needed to promote aid programs to alleviate the plight of the "poorest of the poor."

Prosperity, of course, cannot be bestowed. It must be built on a foundation of self-help and effective government. For some countries, however, external support for their own efforts is essential, much as postwar Europe needed the Marshall Plan. Technical and financial assistance from public and private organizations can encourage sound policies, from environmental protection to more market-oriented development strategies.

The Commission is all too aware that there is little domestic support for foreign aid. In the public mind aid is only a little more popular than "government waste." Yet our foreign aid amounts to less than 0.2 percent of GDP, a smaller percentage than at any time since World War II. Indeed it is the smallest percentage of all among industrial countries.

Table 4: U.S. International Affairs Budget Outlays

(In Millions US$)

	FY 1991 actual	FY 1992 estimated	FY 1993 estimated
Foreign Aid			
Economic & Humanitarian Assistance	4,246	4,750	5,020
Security Assistance	10,060	7,857	7,536
Multilateral Development Banks	1,256	1,571	1,487
International Organizations	1,184	1,567	1,642
Total Foreign Aid	16,746	15,745	15,685
% of U.S. Budget	1.3%	1.1%	1.0%
Other International Affairs	(848)	2,060	2,289
Total International Affairs Budget Outlays	15,898	17,805	17,974

Sources:
Budget of the United States Government, FY93; United Nations Association of the United States of America, "Washington Weekly Report," XVIII (31 January 1992).

Foreign aid is a long-term investment in building the kind of world congenial to our political, security and economic interests. The Commission believes that over the current decade the United States should as a matter of self-interest bring its aid budget into line with those of other industrial nations. Including aid to former Communist countries, reaching such a target is likely to require at least a doubling of our present levels by the year 2000 to $31.5 billion (in 1990 dollars). However, this will be a small sum compared to the decline in our military expenditures.

We must shift U.S. aid policies away from Cold War priorities. Military assistance grants and credits should be substantially reduced or restructured. Developmental, technical, educational, humanitarian and environmental concerns must be given a higher priority.

Today development is being effectively promoted by multilateral financial institutions, including the IMF, the World Bank and regional development banks. Their encouragement of sound market-oriented development policies is responsible for much of the progress being made in developing countries. American support for these institutions has also proven effective in leveraging financial contributions from others.

The Commission believes that continued strong U.S. support for these institutions is essential. We urge both the Administration and Congress to fund future U.S. commitments to them as they become due, rather than stretching contributions out over much longer periods than those of other donors.

We discussed whether a significant U.S. bilateral aid program remains necessary or whether our national interests can be better served by directing our aid through multilateral institutions. We conclude that a bilateral U.S. aid program of moderate size should be maintained.

We agree with the finding of a recent presidential commission that the Agency for International Development (AID) is in need of fundamental reform. But it should not be scrapped. AID has developed valuable programs and skills we will need in future aid efforts. In addition, the United States has special interests of its own – in Central America in the wake of recent civil conflicts and in the Caribbean – that can best be served by retaining our own foreign aid capabilities.

The East Turns to the Market

Some twenty new economies are emerging from the collapse of the Soviet bloc. But their transition from state planning to market-driven policies is proving immensely difficult, a problem of reform that has been described succinctly: "You can make fish soup out of an aquarium, but you can't make an aquarium out of fish soup." Nowhere has the "aquarium problem" been satisfactorily solved. In fact, we are just beginning to comprehend how much economic, environmental and social detritus was left behind by the most massive systemic failure in modern history.

In Eastern Europe initial successes in stabilizing currencies and getting goods to the stores have been followed by rising unemployment and continuing public hardship as state industries fail market tests. Similar problems are occurring in Russia and the other states of the former Soviet Union. The International Labor Organization has warned that in Russia alone unemployment could rise to more than 10 million this year. In all these countries resentment of the newly prosperous few is festering, and fragile democratic political processes are under strain.

The restructuring of physical and human capital will take decades to accomplish. Capital equipment is obsolete, of little market value and lacks basic pollution controls. State industrial enterprises are huge, monopolistic and without critical management and staff resources. While education levels are higher than in developing countries, many basic skills required in a market economy simply do not exist.

A particularly serious problem is the fracture of trading ties among the region's economies. Trade links between Eastern Europe and the Soviet successor states must be reestablished, although on a more market-oriented basis. Equally important is the establishment of commercial trading arrangements within the former Soviet Union. Access to Western markets, also of critical importance, will require both the availability of commercial credit and an openness to the nascent exports of the region.

Notwithstanding determined stabilization and price reform policies, the former Communist states will not overcome their structural problems easily or quickly. Moreover, stabilization programs themselves must to some degree accommodate the credit requirements of inefficient state industries to forestall massive industrial depression. New private enterprises are emerging rapidly, but it will be a long time before they can replace the state sector.

Assisting the Transition

If the countries of the former Soviet bloc can establish functioning market economies in this decade, it would be an historic accomplishment at least equal to the reconstruction of Western Europe and Japan in the 1950s. Such a development would dramatically improve prospects for democracy in the region. It would lay the foundation for a genuine European peace and prosperity that would benefit the world, not least the United States.

Progress toward a market-driven economy is likely to be slow and uneven. It will also be highly dependent on outside support, which must include more than financial and technical assistance. Western markets must be open to Eastern exports, and Western investors must be willing to share capital and know-how.

The Commission strongly endorses a major U.S. commitment to this transition. The United States has taken on such a challenge before and been the better for it. Nowhere, however, have initial conditions been more difficult or more chaotic. We cannot be sure that foreign support will always be well used, particularly in the early stages of the transition. Attaching effective conditions to our assistance can reduce but not eliminate such problems.

Nevertheless, we must bear in mind the huge stake we have in the success of the new democracies. The recent agreement on reducing nuclear arms between Russia and the United States is but one dramatic example.

As with the Marshall Plan, we face more than a call on our generosity for one year or two. There will be no miracles. But America will be a beneficiary if a vast new region of peace, democracy and prosperity emerges.

Since we are at the start of the process, it is important to set out some general principles that can guide our actions and those of other donors:

- **Patience:** Economic transition is going to take at least a decade, with a lot of bumps along the way. We should not look for early results and we should not get alarmed over occasional setbacks.

- **Fairness:** It is important that the process by which assistance is distributed be seen by recipients as reasonable and fair. In the case of the former Soviet Union, aid policies must not become, by design or inertia, a mechanism for reinstituting Russian dominance over the republics.

- **Conditionality:** The political-economic strategies followed by the various recipients must be reasonable and disciplined. These strategies must reflect their determined commitment to the basic principles of a free market, stabilization and privatization. However, it would be counterproductive to require theological conformity. Since donors and recipients alike are learning by experience, a certain variety in strategy and approach is desirable.

- **Self-interest:** Donors should not be shy about emphasizing their interests. Our concern with nuclear proliferation is obvious, as is our desire to limit military expenditures. We also have a legitimate stake in environmental clean-up. The building of democratic systems is essential to all other endeavors.

- **Stewardship:** The IMF and the World Bank play an indispensable role in assisting and evaluating the efforts of both donors and recipients. However, their work is not a substitute for oversight by donor nations. Everything we know about the transition suggests that severe economic, social and political strains are inevitable. Donors and recipients alike will need to understand each other's interests and problems.

Overhauling the System

The policies, institutions and arrangements of the international economic system were put in place more than forty years ago, when the United States was preeminent. Now that this is no longer the case, there is a growing difficulty in elaborating and enforcing multilateral rules governing international trade and finance.

The Commission has concluded that the present system needs a fundamental overhaul. It is disturbing, for example, that nations cannot bring the Uruguay Round to an early conclusion – something so clearly in the interest of all. There are other causes for worry: increased trade protection in industrial countries, the growth of regional arrangements and the inability to develop appropriate norms for monetary policies and exchange rates. We have pointed to the risk that the present system will founder and eventually be replaced by ad hoc arrangements among powerful regions and blocs. Such a development could have serious political and security – as well as economic – consequences.

Even if the worst is avoided, the best the current approach offers is more muddling through. In light of today's stagnant global economy, the prospect of more years of the status quo is cause for alarm.

The United States can no longer by itself lead the way to a stronger international economic system. Collective leadership by the world's major industrial democracies is required. The *Financial Times* summed up the current situation: "Coordination used to mean the U.S. did what it wanted, while everybody else did what the U.S. wanted. Now it means that the major players first argue with one another, whereupon each does precisely what it wants."

The impasse must be broken. The Commission urges the next Administration, as one of its highest priorities, to develop an initiative with the G-7 to promote world growth, revitalize multilateral trade and financial arrangements, encourage the integration of former socialist economies into the global system and support more rapid progress in developing countries.

There should be early agreement both on the scope of the initiative and on the means and timetable to develop and implement it. While the G-7 will wish to consult and to arrange for collaborative efforts with other countries and international institutions, only it can take the lead.

The detailed agenda of such an undertaking would have to be carefully worked out among the parties. Its major elements might include the following:

- A short-term action program to encourage more vigorous global growth, including in particular better coordination of domestic policies by major industrialized countries.

- Agreement on a global trade strategy for the remainder of the decade: an agenda of "new" trade issues to be addressed promptly in post-Uruguay Round trade negotiations; a code of conduct for regional organizations, including provisions for accession by new members; a timetable for the phaseout and elimination of all tariffs and nontariff barriers in industrial countries; and measures for further strengthening GATT as an institution.

- A renewed commitment to develop operating principles of international monetary cooperation, exchange rate management and policy coordination, especially in light of the possible evolution of a European currency. An agreement on exchange rate undertakings – perhaps target zones for key currencies, or fixed but adjustable parities – would be based on commitments to growth, price stability and avoidance of unsustainable external imbalances.

- Agreement on a medium-term strategy of economic and financial support for the countries of Eastern Europe and the former Soviet Union. Such agreement could include the formation of a donors' group with a small permanent staff to coordinate assistance efforts among donors and recipients. We should put in place soon measures to reduce the economic drag of the foreign debts acquired by former Communist states and restore trade among them and with the outside world.

- Development of an action program to help poor countries. This would include bilateral and multilateral funding commitments; early steps to eliminate debt burdens for the poorest countries; and measures to improve access to international financial markets. Our goal should be to assure that developing countries enjoy net inflows of funds.

- Measures to strengthen the G-7, including provision of a small permanent staff, arrangements for closer cooperation with the IMF and other international organizations, and steps leading to its possible evolution into a G-3.

- Review of present institutional arrangements, including the division of responsibilities among the World Bank, the IMF, other international financial organizations and the U.N.

This initiative would build more effective multilateral management of the international economic system. Greater economic parity among North America, East Asia and Europe has caused a sea change in world trade and finance. We have no choice but to move from what was formerly the hegemony of a single country to collective management by the industrial democracies.

Over time we should move toward an even more inclusive global system of economic and financial cooperation. A central concern must be the interests of developing countries, whose futures will have much to say about our own.

"The non-military sources of instability in the economic, social, humanitarian and ecological fields have become threats to peace and security."

*From the summit declaration
by the heads of government of the U.N. Security Council
January 31, 1992*

"The non-military
sources of instability
in the economic, social,
humanitarian and
ecological fields have
become threats
to peace and security."

IV. America's Stake in Global Issues

The Cold War confronted us with a singular threat to our security. Now a multitude of unorthodox challenges to our well-being demand America's urgent attention.

During the past forty years, humans have begun to cause change on a global scale for the first time in history. In our lifetime the world is being transformed by environmental degradation, population growth, migration and humanitarian crises. Addressing these issues raises extraordinarily difficult questions – about the accuracy of scientific projections, the durability of the ecosystem, the morality and methods of population control, the sharing of power through international organizations and the role of American leadership.

Despite continuing debates over these questions, certain ecological and demographic threats are indisputable. Global menaces to an "American way of life" may actually loom larger and more unpredictable in this crowded new world than did the danger of nuclear conflagration during the Cold War. Yet these threats are not unleashed by governments, but by masses of humanity, unmanaged growth and forces of nature.

America's security and economic performance are interwined with the quality of life on earth. Some linkages, like Chernobyl's radiation in the atmosphere, are dramatic. Most, however, do not convey the sense of immediate danger that drives public concern. Only when we understand our personal stake in the global environment will we elevate these issues to the high national priority they require.

Every global issue starts at home – whether that home is in America, Brazil, Poland, Indonesia or Egypt. The state of the world begins with the billions of decisions that citizens, companies, farmers and local governments make every day. So leadership must rest first with the awareness and conscience of men and women. A popular bumper-sticker slogan advises us to "Think globally, act locally." The challenge remains how to convince people that this choice is really theirs to make.

None of our problems is unsolvable. But simply tinkering with existing policies will not suffice. Bold initiatives are essential.

Solutions will not come without controversy and costs. These are threats from which no border can shield us. It is the paradox of this new era that a nation that pursues unilateralism puts its own people at risk. With respect to the environment, as in other areas of global concern, it makes good sense to enter into international agreements with mutual restraints and reciprocal concessions that serve the interests of all.

Protecting a Shared Environment

The population of the world doubled during the Cold War. This explosion, coupled with accelerating technological and economic activity, has placed unprecedented stress on the earth's life support systems. Many measures of human impact – from water use to the emissions of trace gases – show greater change since 1950 than in the previous 10,000 years.

Sound environmental management must be intimately connected to economic growth, not treated as an afterthought. Although there are difficult short-term trade-offs, it is now widely recognized that long-term economic and environmental health are more often mutually dependent than conflicting.

For economic growth to be sustainable over the long term, the costs of environmental and other resources must be taken into account. Market prices frequently do not adequately integrate environmental costs into economic decisions – by either business or government. We should now begin to consider such costs as integral, rather than external, to production.

The shifts required in business practices, government policies and consumer attitudes to reflect a new understanding of "full-cost pricing" pose a major challenge both within and between countries. Such an approach, even if it produces a net social gain, will provoke stiff opposition because it will alter the mix of economic winners and losers.

Other factors contribute to the difficulty of building a consensus for action: scientific uncertainty, the limitations of traditional economic analysis and the unique pressures of trying to cope with irreversible phenomena.

The June 1992 U.N. Conference on Environment and Development in Rio de Janeiro was an unprecedented effort to achieve a global consensus on the priorities of sustainable development. This consensus was not achieved at Rio for many reasons. One important factor was the absence of leadership by the United States.

Nonetheless, the Rio summit created a new agenda. The non-binding *Agenda 21* provides a blueprint for governments, businesses and individuals in the coming years on issues as diverse as fresh water, desertification, hazardous waste, poverty, human health, technology transfer, the advancement of women and population.

Other Rio Summit agreements mark a critical beginning. A non-binding statement of principles on forest management recognizes the critical role of forests in the global environment and discourages deforestation. The biodiversity treaty will help preserve plant and animal species through binding commitments. The climate change treaty commits industrialized nations to adopt policies leading to the stabilizing of greenhouse gas concentrations in the atmosphere and recommends that they reduce their emissions of these gases to 1990 levels as a first step.

Poorer countries see richer ones as principally responsible for past and present environmental degradation. They believe the industrialized nations must act first by reducing their high per capita resource consumption and waste production. They expect additional international assistance to help finance their efforts to protect the environment. But the industrialized nations are only prepared to offer modest amounts. They see the greatest threat to the environment coming from population growth in the developing world.

The Commission believes that this gulf can and must be bridged. The Montreal Protocol of 1987 on stratospheric ozone depletion provides a model. The realization that all countries share a vulnerability to thinning ozone enabled governments, despite scientific uncertainties, to strike a global bargain. The developed nations agreed to act first, reducing their chlorofluorocarbon (CFC) emissions on a tight schedule. They bore the burden of developing substitutes for CFCs and created a modest fund for transfer of the new technologies to developing countries. The latter agreed eventually to eliminate CFCs, but on a much extended schedule and with a period of growth in per capita use allowed in the interim.

Governments agreed at Rio to establish a new Commission on Sustainable Development, which will oversee progress on *Agenda 21* and the other Rio agreements. Most international institutions, however, including the United Nations itself, date from a time when environmental issues had not yet surfaced. Agencies overlap in jurisdiction and fail to coordinate their programs, leaving many major issues untended. The United Nations Environment Programme has a weak charter, is physically isolated in Kenya and is chronically underfunded. More ambitious institutional reform will likely be required before the world can adequately manage the interrelated priorities of environment and development.

The United States, too, must examine its role. Our country is by far the largest consumer of natural resources. Yet the deadlocked domestic debate over energy policy and a reluctance to commit ourselves to multilateral decision making have taken their toll on our ability to lead.

Present U.S. policies on population growth, energy and global warming place us among the laggards, not the leaders, in responding to these issues. Science and self-interest should compel the United States to show the way.

A Crowded Earth

In 1830 world population reached one billion people. Over the next century another billion were added. Today world population grows by a billion every ten years, with more than 90% of the growth in developing countries. Human fertility is declining, but so slowly that the U.N. projects world population to double – under the best assumptions – from the current 5.4 billion to at least 11.2 billion by the end of the next century.

The worst-case scenario? Human population could almost quadruple to 20 billion people by the year 2100.

Population growth, poverty and environmental degradation are closely linked. High levels of investment, modern technology and sound management can make it possible to support more people on a given resource base. High rates of population growth (above 2 percent per year), however, are likely to overwhelm the capacity of most governments to meet basic human needs and to make the necessary investments in job creation and environmental protection. For every Taiwan there is a Bangladesh and a Nigeria with unstable economic and political systems and millions living in wretched conditions.

The rapid growth of the world's population also poses a profound challenge to management of the earth's natural resource base, which is already showing signs of severe stress. Consider, for example, the following U.N. projections of population growth between 1990 and 2025:

Table 5: Projected Population Increases Between 1990 and 2025

(In Millions)

Country	1990	2025
Bangladesh	116	235
Egypt	52	90
Ethiopia	49	127
India	853	1,442
Kenya	24	79
Mexico	89	150
Pakistan	123	267
Zaire	36	99

Source:
U.N. Population Division

Few countries could raise per capita incomes under such pressures. Population growth also threatens international stability as large numbers cross borders in search of work or leave home because land degradation makes it impossible to grow food.

The prescription for defusing the population explosion is economic growth, combined with the education and economic empowerment of women and universal access to family planning services. Although all three are essential to stabilize population growth, the last factor is the least costly and for the years immediately ahead the most pragmatic means to address the issue.

Table 6: Projected Global Population, 1950-2025

(In Billions)

	1950	1992	2000[1]	2025[1]
World (total)	2.5	5.4	6.3	8.5
More Developed Countries	0.8	1.1	1.1	1.2
Less Developed Countries	1.7	4.2	5.1	7.3

Sources: United Nations Population Division, *Long-range World Population Projections*; Population Reference Bureau, Inc., *1992 World Population Data Sheet*.

[1] Future estimates based on the United Nation's medium-variant population projections.

How fast family planning methods spread matters enormously because fertility rates count greatly over a few generations. If a woman bears three children instead of six, and her children and grandchildren do likewise, she will have 27 great-grandchildren rather than 216. If Nigeria, which now has 109 million people, reaches replacement-level fertility by 2010 rather than 2040 (as currently projected), its eventual population would be 341 million, rather than 617 million.

American leadership has been absent on the population crisis for too long. Granted, the United States remains the largest donor (in 1990, $280 million), contributing a substantial percentage of total international funding. Yet the funds remain grossly inadequate to the task and much of the money is misdirected. Since the 1980s the United States has abandoned the two major international organizations devoted to population control efforts: the International Planned Parenthood Federation (outside the Western Hemisphere) and the United Nations Population Fund (UNFPA).

The official reason for denying support for UNFPA – the largest and most effective provider of family planning services – would lead one to believe that the agency is engaged in abortion practices. In fact, UNFPA strongly denies providing support for abortions or abortion-related activities anywhere in the world including China. UNFPA contraception and education programs help prevent large numbers of unwanted pregnancies that would otherwise result in abortions. Ironically U.S. policy has not only meant less education and fewer contraceptives, but more abortions.

In order to meet the U.N.'s lower population projections, UNFPA estimates that the use of family planning services must increase in developing countries to 567 million couples (59 percent of women of reproductive age) by the year 2000, compared with 381 million (51 percent) in 1991. This will require a doubling of total spending on family planning services to $9 billion a year in this decade, $4-5 billion of which would be international aid. This is easily within collective means and is minuscule compared to the benefits.

The American interest is clear. We once again must take global population growth seriously. We need to commit our leadership and resources to a multilateral effort to drastically expand family planning services in the developing world.

The Commission believes that America's principal goal in this area should be to help make access to voluntary family planning services universal by the year 2000. Far more extensive educational programs, particularly for women, will also be critical.

Leadership on Energy

After twenty years of debate America still does not have an effective national energy policy. We have simply left energy to the market, which is far from freely competitive. In the meantime our dependence on imported oil has risen steeply. Our energy productivity (a measure of the amount of energy needed to produce a dollar of GDP) is about half that of Western Europe and Japan. And we face severe obstacles to cleaner air and better transportation systems.

The reasons for our poor performance in energy policy are more political and philosophical than economic. For example, different regions of the U.S. have different energy interests: some are net consumers of energy and some are net producers.

At the Federal level we have focused far more on energy supply than on demand. Yet the economy grew by 40 percent between 1973 and 1986 while energy consumption remained relatively constant because of increasing energy efficiency. But the myth persists in some circles that little can be achieved through further improvements in energy efficiency. In fact much progress has been made in the industrial and transportation sectors. Nationwide, however, our inefficient use of energy adds to our trade deficit, undermines our long-term competitiveness, exposes our economy to abrupt fluctuations of world oil prices, and severely constrains our ability to respond to the threat of greenhouse warming.

The Commission believes that the United States should, as a matter of national priority, substantially raise our energy productivity over the next decade. We need to close the gap between our performance and the levels already achieved by Japan and Western Europe. Doing so would enhance long-term domestic economic renewal and bring substantial foreign policy gains.

Price is the key. Energy prices are determined largely by the price of oil, which in the United States is used mostly for transportation. The real price of gasoline in the United States today is lower than at any time since 1947. The tax our consumers pay on gasoline is far lower than most of the rest of the world, only one-eighth the level in Europe, one-quarter that of Japan and half that of Canada. Cheap energy is appealing in the short term, but the long-term costs are enormous. Higher energy prices in these other countries mean that energy efficiency receives greater priority when companies build new plants, new communities are planned and individuals make decisions about daily transportation.

Comparative Gasoline Prices and Taxes

(U.S. Dollars/Gallon)

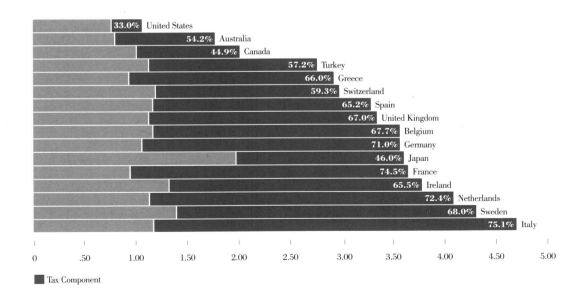

Source: OECD

The Commission believes that raising energy prices through higher taxes rather than more government regulation is the most efficient way to achieve greater energy productivity. We recommend, therefore, that the United States progressively implement a series of substantial taxes on gasoline (illustratively up to $1/gallon) and other petroleum products; on automobiles (a weight tax according to fuel efficiency); and on carbon content.

A substantial gain in American energy productivity will limit our growing dependence on imported oil and thus strengthen our national security. It will greatly enhance our efforts to reduce greenhouse gas emissions and improve the quality of our environment. Energy taxes would also produce substantial new revenues that could be used to reduce the deficit, rebuild infrastructure and meet other urgent priorities.

We are well aware of the political difficulty of this proposal. An energy tax program will have to be carefully designed to cushion its impact on lower income consumers. It will also have to be phased in over a number of years to permit adjustment on the part of industry and the public. However, we are convinced that greater efficiency in energy use is essential for the United States. Higher energy prices are unavoidable.

Regulation can also play a role in some areas, by encouraging the shift to vehicles powered by electricity, compressed natural gas and, in the long run, hydrogen. Greater use of natural gas, the cleanest fossil fuel, is a high priority. So is the rationalization of a transportation policy that promotes the use of the motor vehicle over all other options.

Over the long term nuclear power remains an important energy option, but only after full exploitation of cost-effective improvements in our use of conventional energy and development of economically competitive renewable energy sources. Sensible but scrupulous regulation, a solid safety record and an operating waste disposal system are preconditions for a revival of nuclear power plant construction. A waste disposal plan, which would be necessary even if another nuclear plant were never built, is the most pressing need.

The Warming Earth

There is still a measure of uncertainty in our understanding of the so-called greenhouse effect. Continuing emissions of greenhouse gases (principally carbon dioxide, methane and CFCs) ultimately will cause average global temperatures to rise, precipitation patterns to shift and other major changes in climate. However, there are many unknowns, especially the role of the oceans and clouds in the development of a greenhouse effect, the amount of temperature increase that can be expected under given conditions over a given period of time and the regional effects of climate change.

That these uncertainties exist is not surprising. The forces that create the global climate are complex, and its study began only recently. Further advances in scientific understanding – and further surprises, like the discovery of the Antarctic ozone hole in 1985 – are certain.

The past year, for example, saw a major development in understanding the role of CFCs. Until then, they were thought to account for as much as one-quarter of present warming. But it was discovered that ozone loss also has a cooling impact. The two effects of CFCs – warming through their greenhouse properties and cooling through ozone loss – are about equal in magnitude. Thus CFCs are now believed to cause no net warming.

Table 7: Greenhouse Gas Emissions

(Percent Shares)

Country	Percent
United States	17.3
Former USSR	14.0
EC	11.2
China	9.3
Japan	4.9
India	4.7
Brazil	4.6
Mexico	1.9
Indonesia	1.7
Canada	1.7

Source:
World Resources Institute, 1989

The Commission discussed the issue of greenhouse warming at length. More greenhouse gases in the atmosphere will certainly change the world's climate. The uncertainties are how much and how fast. Many members of the Commission believe the scientific case for the emergence of a substantial, and possibly devastating, greenhouse effect by the middle of the next century has been made. Others believe that firm conclusions must await further scientific study.

We all agree, however, that there are good and urgent reasons for action now. Prudence dictates prompt efforts to reduce the risk of long-term irreversible climate change, the impact of which might range from moderate to catastrophic, especially when the economic costs are modest.

Policy measures must be quickly put in place to stabilize and, if necessary, reduce emissions of carbon dioxide and other greenhouse gases into the earth's atmosphere. In effect, we need insurance against future contingencies. As time passes, decisions about how much insurance to buy will depend upon the information that becomes available on climatic risk and the resources we are willing to devote to reduce this risk.

America could substantially decrease some of its greenhouse gas emissions at low cost or with even a net gain to the economy. With the exception of the United States, all OECD states have pledged to reduce their carbon dioxide emissions to 1990 levels by the year 2000. Several have pledged deep cuts. Numerous studies suggest the feasibility of the United States lowering its emissions to the 1990 level by the end of the decade and sustaining it for some thirty years. The energy taxes the Commission advocates should help make this a realistic target. As the need for further reduction of emissions becomes clear, additional legislation should be enacted.

Once again America needs to act jointly with others. Even concerted action by all the industrialized nations, however, could not succeed without comparable moves by the developing world. International cooperation is imperative and, as the global warming treaty signed in Rio demonstrates, attainable. Negotiation of a far-reaching treaty in just three years, even one without emission reduction timetables and targets, is a striking achievement.

The United States, the world's largest emitter of greenhouse gases, bears an unavoidable responsibility to support, facilitate and encourage multilateral action. The Commission urges swift ratification of the global warming treaty, followed by negotiation of protocols guiding the pace and degree of reduction needed for the management of greenhouse gases. As scientific progress enhances our understanding of the global climate and the greenhouse effect, these agreements can be modified – much the same way we have strengthened the original Vienna convention and Montreal protocol on protection of the ozone layer.

We should join others in committing to a steady, long-term course of reducing the risks of global climate change.

It is particularly important that the United States provide major developing countries – such as Brazil, Nigeria, India, China and Mexico – technical assistance in the efficient production and use of energy.

People on the Move

The international movement of people – voluntarily as legal or illegal migrants and involuntarily as refugees – has emerged as one of the most complex and volatile issues of the post-Cold War era. At the end of 1991 there were more than 18 million refugees,

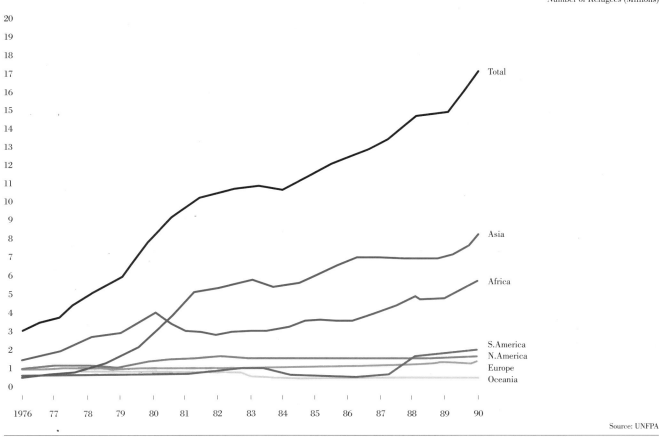

Number of Refugees (Millions)

20
19
18
17 — Total
16
15
14
13
12
11
10
9
8 — Asia
7
6 — Africa
5
4
3
2 — S.America
1 — N.America
0 — Europe
— Oceania

1976 77 78 79 80 81 82 83 84 85 86 87 88 89 90

Source: UNFPA

millions of regular immigrants and countless illegal immigrants around the world. Western countries now spend about $7 billion a year simply on support of asylum seekers within their borders. The number of people who are internally displaced – civilians uprooted within their own lands – is estimated to exceed 20 million.

In many countries immigration is causing great economic stress and building intense political pressures. The situation will get much worse before it gets better. Western European nations, for example, are already alarmed about current and potential immigration flows, and anti-immigrant feeling is growing sharply. The destruction of Yugoslavia has created the largest displacement of persons in Europe since World War II. In Africa migrations triggered by armed conflicts and environmental disasters have imposed enormous strains on impoverished nations. Poorer countries continue to suffer the loss of many of their best people.

Americans should be among the first to understand the forces at work in migration flows. After all, ours is a nation of immigrants who fled their countries for reasons as diverse as economic hardship, political persecution, war and the lack of religious freedom.

Immigration is once again changing America. The 1980s was the largest immigration decade in our history. The trend is continuing in the nineties. Today's newcomers are no longer largely from Europe, but overwhelmingly from Latin America and Asia, broadening America's ethnic diversity in unprecedented ways.

The continual infusion of new Americans immeasurably enriches our nation. It adds a largely young, productive element and new dynamism to what is already the most diverse society on earth.

Yet large-scale immigration also brings serious problems of adjustment, social tensions and financial costs. Americans are feeling the impact of large numbers of immigrants as pressures for schools, housing, jobs and English language instruction increase.

The demands on financial support for the domestic resettlement of refugees have grown. A number of state governments – from California to Florida to New York – are facing heavy costs in meeting the social service needs of immigrants.

Political and economic factors are generating greater population flows around the world. Wars and civil strife produced millions of refugees from Indochina, Afghanistan and Africa. Asylum seekers came from Eastern Europe, Central America and the Caribbean. During the 1980s, the economic gains of the previous decade in the developing world slowed or were reversed. Coupled with high birth rates in the 1950s and 1960s, unprecedented numbers of new workers poured into the labor markets. Inevitably, South-North migration accelerated as people moved in search of jobs. Much of it has been illegal.

Migration follows patterns established by history, labor recruitment and economic penetration. Once migration footholds are secured, family members follow, remittances bind communities across great distances and old immigrant groups help new ones. Migration becomes not only a new link between nations but also itself a stimulus to more migration.

Taken together, these trends are not diminishing, but deepening, embedded in the conditions of our world. Regulated immigration continues to make important contributions to the economy and life of this country. However, migration is not the answer to population and economic pressures in poor countries. Nor are immigration opportunities in the United States and other developed nations an acceptable way to meet the employment needs of the rest of the world.

Over the long term economic growth and low fertility rates are indispensable. In the short term our efforts should be directed at reducing the life-threatening circumstances that cause mass migrations, developing strategies that protect peoples' right to stay or return home in safety and establishing better mechanisms to channel flows that are inevitable.

The Commission believes that migration is one of the most pressing problems of the post-Cold War era. A comprehensive multilateral agenda should be addressed in:

- **International law:** Traditional rules defining refugees are inadequate because increasingly migrants do not fit the definition – a victim of political persecution – set forth in the 1951 Refugee Convention. An instrument born of Europe's post-World War II experience, the Convention fails to allow for victims of war, economic and political disintegration or environmental disaster. It needs to be comprehensively updated – a difficult, multiyear effort.

- **Finances:** The U.N. High Commission for Refugees (UNHCR), the lead agency for international refugee relief, operates almost entirely on voluntary contributions from member-states. As the largest contributor, the United States must maintain high levels of support and the budget flexibility to respond to UNHCR needs. We must also continue the effort to make refugees a more broadly shared financial responsibility.

- **Voluntary repatriation:** Most refugees or displaced persons want to go home. As conflicts generated by the Cold War have receded, repatriation has become possible for millions. Every effort should be made to get them out of camps so they can return. That may necessitate concerted international efforts in diplomacy, peacekeeping, democratization, economic development and environmental restoration to create the necessary conditions for refugees to go home. Repatriation is expensive but far less costly than resettlement abroad.

- **The right to stay:** During the Cold War, we celebrated the right to leave. Now we must promote the right to stay. This right to stay in one's own land with certain guarantees of human rights should become a staple of international life. The international community must develop the means to evaluate the policies of countries that generate migrations and, where appropriate, take steps to bring about change.

The Humanitarian Imperative

The cost of the Cold War was captured in compelling human images: the Vietnamese and Cuban boat people, the maimed children of Afghanistan, young East Germans sprinting for freedom.

Large-scale human disasters also burden much of today's world. Only the actors are different – Haitians for Cubans, Bosnians for Afghans. Humanitarian crises are immediate; often they are manmade. We must try not only to react to them but also to prevent them. If we do, we can save lives and we can save money.

Take Africa, for example, the locus of many disasters. Most African countries are under growing strain from ruinous economic policies, drought, depressed commodity prices, ethnic conflict, refugees, AIDS and population pressures.

There are a few rays of hope. South Africa's progress toward a multiracial political settlement – however difficult – enhances prospects for stability and economic advancement in all of Southern Africa. Increasing receptivity to market-oriented economic policies in many African countries holds promise for greater growth. And more democratic systems have emerged in parts of the continent.

But there is a long way to go. Unless we can help build a better foundation for development in Africa, the degradation of the environment, internal conflicts and mass movements of peoples will inevitably lead to greater human tragedies and impose even larger costs on us and the world community.

For Africa and elsewhere, much of the day-to-day business of America's foreign policy comes down to how we respond to another disaster, the latest surge of refugees, the devastation of a typhoon and the death and destruction from civil war.

All nations have a concern with the plight of large numbers of people trapped within a country or streaming across its borders. No government has the right to forcibly export its peoples to other countries or make them refugees in their own.

The allied military intervention into northern Iraq to assist the Kurds in 1991 set the stage for new approaches to humanitarian crises. Threats to peace and security are being broadened to include such crises, allowing the U.N. Security Council to respond with sanctions or military force if necessary. Humanitarian crises can cover many situations, including the inability to peacefully deliver assistance to civilians, the brutal expulsion of ethnic minorities and internal aggression against whole populations. At the United Nations and in regional organizations, important initiatives are underway that will establish a new doctrine of humanitarian intervention.

The United States has not and must not stand aloof from the humanitarian calamities of our times. American leadership is essential to quickly and effectively crafting both regional and international initiatives. A new principle of international relations is arising: the destruction or displacement of large groups of people within states justifies international intervention. A new balance must be struck between traditional sovereignty and the world community's interest in human rights.

The United States must be prepared, together with other countries, to engage in various forms of intervention, including forcible ones requiring U.S. military power. "Forcible" does not necessarily mean armed combat. Some humanitarian operations can be successful with a show of force intended to protect international aid personnel. The use of U.N. forces (sometimes heavily armed) to facilitate delivery of humanitarian aid can help fulfill this purpose. The creation of safe land or air corridors can also achieve humanitarian objectives. The circumstances of each operation necessarily determine the manner and size of intervention. In some cases military action may be the only alternative.

The United States should be more actively engaged in strengthening the collective machinery to carry out humanitarian actions. In this way we can reduce the likelihood of having to choose between unilateral military intervention and standing idle in the face of human tragedy.

Drugs: A Menace from Home

The United States has the highest rate of drug abuse of any industrialized country in the world. By one measure, America has five percent of the world's population and consumes fifty percent of the world's cocaine. Twenty-six million Americans reported using illicit drugs during 1991. Almost half acknowledged using drugs at least once a month. Forty-four percent of all American teenagers try illicit drugs before they finish high school.

Efforts to cut off the supply of drugs as close to the source as possible have dominated U.S. drug policy for decades. The assumption is that curtailing drug availability will drive up prices, forcing drug users to stop or to seek treatment. This approach has never worked.

The progress we have made in combatting drug abuse is a result not of reduced supply, but of reduced demand. New approaches to prevention, treatment and community law enforcement are showing positive results. Yet the U.S. government continues to rely heavily on international control and interdiction, spending almost as much in 1992 for these programs as the nation spends on all domestic drug prevention, education and treatment combined.

In fact, international efforts have failed to curtail the availability of drugs in this country but have contributed to political instability in countries where powerful drug smugglers threaten governments, most notably in Peru. U.S. narcotics assistance programs abroad often foster human rights abuses and corruption among foreign police and military officials.

After decades of blaming other countries for our drug problems, the United States simply must start taking responsibility at home. We have learned a great deal about reducing drug abuse and crime, but we have not yet begun to apply what we know on a national scale.

There is, of course, room for some international drug control cooperation as well. But we reject the current approach that makes foreign bilateral programs the centerpiece of our drug policy. Reducing worldwide illicit drug trafficking will require global efforts, but U.S. support for multilateral cooperation of this sort has been minimal. The average U.S. contribution to the U.N. drug agencies has remained under $5 million a year since 1977. We need to increase that figure.

In the wake of America's victory in Operation Desert Storm, we can expect some to argue for increased reliance on the military to win the war on drugs. To many such a campaign may prove politically and emotionally appealing. But this is not an appropriate way of justifying defense expenditures. And such a strategy only postpones the day when we are forced to admit that the enemy is not in foreign capitals, but in our own neighborhoods.

In the war against drugs, like so much else on our national agenda, it is time to wage the battle at home. We must reduce demand.

Strengthening International Organizations

The Commission emphasizes throughout this report that greater use of collective efforts must be part of a new kind of American leadership. Most major international institutions were conceived during and immediately after World War II. They reached maturity during the Cold War. The Commission seriously questions whether, as presently constituted, they are meeting the new needs of the international community.

- **A New Dumbarton Oaks:** In the wake of World War II, a new future for international organizations was developed at Dumbarton Oaks. After half a century the world needs a new Dumbarton Oaks.

    In Chapter V, we stress the importance of strengthening the capacity of the United Nations to meet growing requirements for peacekeeping and enforcement operations. In Chapter III, we press the need for an overhaul of the major international economic institutions.

    The enormity of the task of organizing for more effective multilateral action leads us to propose that the United States initiate an international assessment of the family of U.N. agencies and other major multilateral organizations. This assessment should include a reexamination of the rationale for each organization, the assignment of responsibilities among them and the possible revision of their charters.

- **The U.N. Security Council:** The U.N. Charter needs revision to eliminate outdated provisions and better match new realities. One critical area of reform is the antiquated structure of the Security Council. If the Council is to function as a kind of international executive committee, its permanent membership cannot remain frozen in a post-World War II snapshot of the world. While we do not underestimate the political difficulties involved in changing the current structure, we believe the Council's permanent membership should reflect the economic weight and political responsibility of the world's major states.

    As a first order change, Japan and Germany should become permanent members. Germany will need to coordinate with the other European members of the Security Council so that the European component of the Council is representative. Some of the leading countries in the developing world may also need to be accommodated.

    Until the Charter can be amended, the United States should consult regularly with Japan, Germany and the European Community on all important issues before the Security Council.

- **General U.N. Financing Issues:** The international community is dumping the most intractable and complex problems of the new world on the United Nations without contributing the necessary funds. The financial burdens of the United Nations and its agencies will only deepen as peacekeeping, refugee, disaster relief and environmental costs mount. Many authorized and projected U.N. peacekeeping operations cannot be undertaken without a basic change in the attitudes and commitments of major donors.

For many years now the United States has had the dubious distinction of being the largest U.N. debtor. During fiscal year 1993, the expected U.S. outlays for all U.N. activities constitute less than one-tenth of one percent of the federal budget. In fact, our contributions to the regular budget of the United Nations and its agencies (excluding peacekeeping and arrearages) will be less than $700 million, the annual budget of the New York City Fire Department.

Any plausible vision for America's future role in the world must include a renewed financial commitment to the United Nations. The United States is assessed 25 percent of the regular U.N. budget and 30.4 percent of the regular U.N. peacekeeping budget. These assessments are treaty obligations and should be distinguished from the other components of the annual U.S. foreign aid budget that are discretionary.

We recommend reducing the U.S. peacekeeping assessment from its current level to 25 percent. This move would increase assessments for other major industrialized countries on an equitable basis. In return, the United States must clean up its own budgetary process so that it pays all U.N. arrearages promptly and, in the future, makes its assessed payments on time.

A bold but pragmatic set of financing proposals has been put forward by the U.N. Secretary-General in his recent report to the Security Council, *An Agenda for Peace.* The proposals include charging interest on arrearages, increasing the U.N.'s working capital fund, establishing more reliable funding mechanisms for peacekeeping and authorizing the Secretary-General to borrow commercially if necessary. The Secretary-General has also invited changes in the formula for calculating assessments for peacekeeping operations.

The Commission has not had the opportunity to examine each of these proposals. Several appear to have merit, however, and we urge policymakers to study them carefully.

The United Nations faces a full and urgent agenda. Helping ensure that it can carry out that agenda will test America's commitment to collective leadership.

Why are the streets and squares emptying
so rapidly, everyone going home lost in thoughts?

Because night has fallen,
and the Barbarians have not come.

And some of our men, just in from the border,
say there are no Barbarians any longer!

Now, what is going to happen to us without
the Barbarians? They were, those people, after all,
a kind of solution.

C.P. Cavafy
From a poem about ancient Alexandria

Why this bewilderment?
This sudden confusion?

Why are the streets and squares emptying
so rapidly, everyone going home lost in thoughts?

Because night has fallen,
and the Barbarians have not come.

And some of our men, just in from the border,
say there are no Barbarians any longer!

Now, what is going to happen to us without
the Barbarians? They were, those people, after all,
a kind of solution.

C.P. Cavafy
From a poem about ancient Alexandria

V. Beyond the Cold War

The ancients strived to keep the barbarians at the gate. For half a century America strived to contain Communism within its vast Eurasian empire.

Containment, born in the Truman Administration, was the watchword for three generations of Americans. Between 1946 and 1991 taxpayers spent nearly five trillion dollars on defense, about six percent of the country's production. While all Americans sacrificed at home, millions put themselves in harm's way abroad. Tens of thousands perished in the highlands of Korea and the jungles of Vietnam.

Containment is perhaps the greatest example in American history of a long-term bipartisan policy successfully defined, pursued and achieved. But a secret of its success was its very singularity – its focused determination to protect the West from Communist expansionism. Other efforts – whether to halt nuclear proliferation, promote democracy or improve the competitive position of American industries and workers – took a back seat.

Now that the Cold War is over, we are free to move away from a peace that rests on a balance of terror between two armed camps toward a peace based on trust and shared interest.

This kind of peace is real, not utopian. It will be difficult to achieve. But it can be seen in the interwoven ties of commerce, culture and shared values that already bind the democracies of North America, Western Europe and Japan. There is room for diversity and disagreement in such a peace, but within the bounds of mutual respect. Established procedures insure that conflicts are resolved peacefully without recourse to violence. No country is so poor in spirit, so forsaken by history that it cannot aspire one day to join this rich tapestry of nations.

To advance such a peace:

- The United States must remain the world's leading military power – engaged, although more selectively, in security efforts where our interests require. This is still a necessary condition for a durable peace – but it is insufficient.

- Whenever possible, we must act cooperatively with others while retaining the option of unilateral action. Toward this end, the system of global collective security designed by the founders of the United Nations should be strengthened to reflect new opportunities and reinforced by regional collective security arrangements.

- The world's resources devoted to military forces and equipment must be substantially cut. Above all, we must continue to reduce weapons of mass destruction and strengthen efforts to block their proliferation.

America: The Leading Military Power

The unrelenting mortal threat to our national security has been lifted. While Russia retains residual nuclear forces which can devastate America, the disintegration of the Soviet Union's military machine can only be considered a windfall for U.S. security. Rebuilding the Soviet military threat or building a similar threat in another country would take years, sufficient time for it to be detected and countered.

But we still live in a violent and uncertain world. Nationalism is fueling a growing number of dangerous conflicts and redrawing maps. Bloody battles rage in Africa, Asia, Latin America and now in Europe. Thousands of nuclear-armed missiles and aircraft, capable of reaching the United States, remain on the territory of the former Soviet Union, on the high seas and in a few other countries. And we must not forget that there are countries still openly hostile toward the United States. Some, like North Korea, threaten our friends. Others, like Libya, sponsor terrorists who threaten Americans around the world.

Worse, several nations are developing nuclear, chemical or biological weapons. A few, like Syria, already have chemical capabilities, possibly mated with the missiles to deliver them. Still others, like Iran and Iraq, seek to acquire both conventional and unconventional military power sufficient to dominate particular regions and thereby harm American interests.

The United States is the world's leading military power. We must keep it that way. No nation should ever be allowed to threaten the world the way the Soviet Union did. While U.S. military involvement can be more selective than when we had an enemy with global reach, we need to remain prepared for the unknown. U.S. military strength will also remain the backbone of collective responses to serious threats.

America's armed forces must do more than defend our interests from direct threats. They must also support our diplomacy, lending weight to our initiatives and helping shape how other countries see us. U.S. military power is a factor in the calculations of decision makers throughout the world. If our armed forces were unable to respond to threats to our interests far from our shores, the world would become more unpredictable and dangerous.

Yet, with the demise of the Soviet military machine, U.S. preeminence is so great that we can make large cuts in our armed forces and still remain the leading military power. We also can progressively withdraw most of our forces deployed abroad while restructuring our security roles in Europe, East Asia and the Pacific.

Europe

During the Cold War the United States was central to a security order in Europe that contained Soviet power, muted historic European conflicts and promoted intense collaboration among our allies. Our vital stake in assuring that Western Europe was not dominated by a country or combination of countries hostile to American interests was well served.

These underpinnings have been fundamentally altered. NATO and the American troop presence as currently structured do not address Europe's most pressing security problems. Threats to peace in Europe are most likely to erupt from ethnic conflicts within states and from the clashes they may cause between neighboring countries. Yugoslavia is only the most compelling case of the new threats to European security. Military conflicts have already broken out in some Soviet successor states. More are likely. The continuing presence of nuclear weapons in some of these new countries creates a special set of worries.

This new landscape challenges the United States to work with our European partners to devise collective solutions to these new problems of regional security.

The North Atlantic Treaty Organization (NATO) is the foundation for a continuing American security role in Europe. NATO, however, must be redefined. In its mission, internal structure and planning, NATO is mismatched with Europe's new security problems. Both the alliance and the American military presence will be maintained by American taxpayers and European voters only if they are relevant to contemporary realities.

One purpose of a revised NATO and continued American participation in European security affairs should be to deter the emergence of a new military threat from the East. With American leadership, NATO can forge relationships with the new democracies in the eastern part of the continent, helping them reduce their armed forces and military industries while seeking to convey a greater sense of security to their leaders and people. The newly formed North Atlantic Cooperation Council (NACC) joins the North Atlantic Treaty Organization with the nations that once made up the territory of the Warsaw Pact. The Council can facilitate military collaboration among former enemies.

NATO also remains important to Germany. Through NATO Germany retains a voice on nuclear decisions it would not have otherwise, and thus has little interest in acquiring its own nuclear capabilities. Germany's strong multilateral engagement stems in part from its perception that the United States and other European partners continue to be committed to collective undertakings. We have a direct interest in reassuring Germany that it can rely on the alliance for its security. The American presence also reassures Germany's neighbors, who are closely watching the evolution of German policy.

The Commission welcomes NATO's decision to work with other European institutions, and particularly with the Conference on Security and Cooperation in Europe (CSCE), in a peacekeeping role in Eastern Europe and the Soviet successor states.

NATO can provide the military and logistical capabilities necessary to enable distrustful and warring parties to reach cease-fires, territorial accommodations and political settlements. If political and diplomatic efforts organized by the CSCE, the United Nations or other organizations set the stage, NATO peacekeeping forces could contribute to the resolution of ethnic conflicts in the Balkans and elsewhere in Eastern Europe. NATO personnel could monitor and ensure compliance with cease-fires, help disarm irregular forces, investigate charges of truce violations and provide humanitarian relief.

There was disagreement within the Commission on whether it is sufficient to give NATO only a peacekeeping role in Eastern Europe and the former Soviet Union. Some propose that NATO go further and take on greater security commitments – even to the point of deploying military forces in hostile situations to suppress violence and establish cease-fires. Other members consider this to be an excessive political leap for NATO and for the United States. It would mean placing Americans and West Europeans in harm's way in the interest of East European stability.

Most of us, however, do favor another new role for NATO – an extension of its focus to the Middle East and Persian Gulf regions. There is no doubt that cooperative Western military interventions in the region, if necessary, could be greatly strengthened if they could take advantage of NATO's planning and logistical apparatus, to say nothing of its integrated commands and forces. But we recognize that such joint actions will be difficult. U.S. and European perceptions of their national interests in the region differ in significant ways. During the Gulf War, for example, NATO allies deployed their forces to the region individually and cobbled together a military coalition on the spot. At a minimum, joint NATO actions outside Europe will require far closer cooperation and far more sharing of decisions than in the past.

Regardless of its new missions, there should be major changes in NATO's internal structure and military posture. European members should assume a proportionate role in the Alliance's decision-making processes, reflecting the changed nature of threats to regional security and the greater equality that now characterizes the trans-Atlantic relationship.

In order to build a broader base for collective security on the continent, NATO should also consider accepting new members. Membership in a refurbished NATO, for instance, could require such standards as a democratic form of government, adherence to the rule of law, renunciation of territorial claims, commitment to protect individual human rights, the willingness and capability to offer mutual assistance to other member states and perhaps acceptance of something less than a full veto for a transition period.

There is a multiplicity of security institutions in the new Europe. NATO, the European Community, the Conference on Security and Cooperation in Europe, the West European Union and other organizations are all playing a role in the emerging security structure. This diversity is untidy and duplicative, but in itself it is not damaging to American interests. Given the political diversity of Europe, no one institution, not even NATO, can carry the entire weight of providing for European security.

It was the United States, after all, that urged the establishment of a fully integrated European army forty years ago in the form of the European Defense Community. Successive American administrations pressed Europeans to intensify their military cooperation. So the United States should welcome the fulfillment by Europeans of a long-term U.S. goal – strengthening multilateral security structures.

The enhancement of European military cooperation within the West European Union may be the most effective way to achieve this goal. However the Europeans choose to organize themselves, it is important for the United States and the Europeans to ensure that the new structures complement, rather than compete with, the Atlantic Alliance. We must discard a dogmatic NATO-or-nothing approach.

The radically changed security environment in Europe also means that substantial reductions can be made in the U.S. military presence. Some American troops should remain there as long as they are wanted by our allies, but they should consist primarily of naval and air forces and a modest ground element including the logistical and administrative resources necessary for rapid reinforcement. The Bush Administration has already proposed to cut in half the 300,000 U.S. troops that have been deployed in Europe and indicated recently a willingness to go even further. Most of us agree that over the next several years further reductions can and should be made.

Asia and the Pacific

Strong economic growth is changing the Pacific region. Spreading networks of trade and investment are binding Asian nations to one another and moderating historical animosities. Taiwan is investing in China, Thailand in Indochina, Korea in Russia and Japan everywhere.

Together with the lifting of the Soviet threat and the decline of Communism, these new ties within Asia have fundamentally changed the security environment. With the withdrawal of Vietnam from Cambodia the only real confrontation left in the region is between North and South Korea.

Nevertheless, the nations of the area harbor lingering security concerns. Because of their size and capabilities, Japan and China loom as the main potential threats to most countries in the region. By virtue of geography and history the United States is not viewed in this way. Virtually all countries, particularly Japan, want the United States to maintain a military presence, although not necessarily at the current level.

There are major unknowns that affect the whole region. The coming changes in China's leadership raise basic questions about that country's future direction, even the stability and effectiveness of the central government. The division of Korea may be approaching its end, but the process could be chaotic. North Korea's attempt to produce nuclear weapons adds a major unsettling factor. Territorial disputes remain throughout the area, including those between Japan and Russia over the Northern Islands, and among many nations, including China, over islands in the South China Sea.

While we can continue to remove progressively many of the 125,000 Americans stationed in East Asia, we should keep naval forces in the Western Pacific, retain some U.S. forces in Japan and maintain a combat-ready presence in South Korea until a peaceful resolution of the Korean division is achieved. We must not give up our stake in the world's most dynamic region.

Nothing can replace a close security relationship with Japan as the cornerstone of Pacific stability and American security. Japan's already strong role in Asia will only grow with its increasing economic weight. It is in our interest – as well as Japan's – that this role evolve in the context of a collaborative relationship. Our national security interests in the region would be endangered by a divergence between us and Japan. Such a rift might prompt Japan – the only major non-nuclear power in Northeast Asia – to conclude that it could no longer rely on the American security commitment and reassess its own military posture. A remilitarized Japan would be devastating to regional stability.

Notwithstanding the disappearance of the Soviet threat, China will be very important to American interests. With its huge population, nuclear weapons, permanent Security Council seat, rapidly growing market and impact on regional and global issues, China will be one of the central world actors of the next century.

As long as a repressive regime rules in Beijing, America will have trouble defining a policy that reflects our values yet preserves long-term ties. We should pursue a businesslike relationship, one that maintains dialogue on major international and bilateral topics, including economic, non-proliferation and regional issues. At the same time we should vigorously press our human rights concerns, avoiding a double standard that contrasts with our global position.

We should continue selective sanctions with regard to China, including the one on military cooperation. On the other hand we should maintain economic, cultural, scientific and academic links to encourage progressive forces there. A majority of Commission members also believe that maintaining Most Favored Nation treatment for China promotes reform, avoids hurting the wrong targets and serves our long-term interests.

If and when a more moderate government emerges in China, we should move rapidly to restore and strengthen the full range of our relations.

In Southeast Asia and South Asia, our interests are now mostly, though not exclusively, economic. The Commission believes we must be prepared to contribute our full share to the cost of U.N.-led efforts to bring about a political settlement in Cambodia. We should also normalize our relations with Vietnam. We view nuclear non-proliferation objectives in India and Pakistan as particularly urgent. The end of the Cold War offers new opportunities for strengthening our ties with India, particularly as New Delhi proceeds with economic reform.

The Middle East

The United States has more influence in the Middle East than ever. We and our allies – Israel, Turkey, Saudi Arabia and Egypt – have a strong position. The principal threats – Iraq, Iran and to a lesser extent Syria – are in difficult circumstances and their prospects are uncertain. No single power threatens our oil supply. The removal of Soviet influence, the outcome of the Gulf War and the results of the June 1992 elections in Israel have opened new opportunities for reducing Arab-Israeli hostility and resolving the Palestinian issue. Our freedom to take the initiative has risen significantly.

The threats to our Arab partners as well as to the stability of oil prices are in fact primarily internal. They include governmental weakness in Gulf states, Islamic fundamentalism, as well as poverty and economic difficulties in most Arab countries. The prospects for managing these problems are uneven. Success in limiting our dependence on imported oil would of course reduce our vulnerability.

But there are also new concerns. Most serious is the proliferation of weapons of mass destruction in Syria, Iran and Iraq, which we discuss later. The emergence of five new Central Asian nations and three new nations in the Caucasus has changed the geography of the region. Ethnic conflicts abound. These states are weak economically, and in some cases their cohesion is in doubt. They could easily become the objects of struggles for influence among regional powers.

Iran will always be a major power in the Gulf and an important actor in Central Asia because of its size, location and oil. However, Iranian hegemony over the region would seriously challenge American interests. We must be prepared to confront it with the full range of instruments at our disposal. If, on the other hand, the regime in Teheran genuinely begins to develop a less confrontational posture toward the West, we should be prepared to respond carefully, building a businesslike relationship and encouraging change. In either case we should join our allies in supporting Turkey as a counterweight to Iran.

We must be prepared for ongoing instability throughout the region, particularly in the Gulf. Whether or not instability leads to armed conflicts, the United States must retain the capability to project superior military forces into the area to protect our interests. However, other countries also have a major stake in an assured flow of Gulf oil at stable, predictable prices. Although we will remain the principal guarantor of security in the Gulf, we should pursue collective policies that involve Europe and Japan.

Israel remains a good friend of the United States. We must maintain both our firm commitment to Israel's security and our long-term strategic interest in good relations with moderate Arab governments. No other government can take our place in promoting peace in the region through direct negotiations.

The best hope for Arab-Israeli progress toward a more peaceful region lies in interim steps that are negotiable. Such agreements hold the promise of gradually building the mutual trust needed to achieve a durable peace. Such progress will require persistent American diplomacy over many years.

U.S. Military Posture and the Defense Budget

America no longer needs many permanent bases overseas. Some American forces should be retained in Europe and East Asia. Elsewhere, however, we can rely on agreements that permit us to station equipment close to the scenes of potential conflict, like the Persian Gulf. This would facilitate the rapid movement of troops and arms in a crisis.

The bulk of U.S. armed forces should be based in the United States, and be organized and equipped so that they can be deployed anywhere in the world on short notice and sustained overseas as long as necessary. Structuring forces in this manner is more expensive than keeping them overseas. It means a greater emphasis on air and sea lift, on lighter, flexible combat forces, on space-based surveillance and command, control and communications systems and on the equipment and support forces that make it possible to quickly move ground, air and sea forces.

Some nations hostile to the United States as well as our allies are likely to continue to acquire weapons of mass destruction and the ability to deliver these weapons at long range by ballistic missiles, aircraft, and other means. Accordingly, the United States should continue to develop defensive technologies. To protect United States and allied forces abroad, the acquisition of effective defenses against tactical ballistic missiles should proceed. Once cost-effective technologies to defend against intercontinental ballistic missiles are available, consideration should be given to deploying these defensive systems. Such deployments might require modification of the ABM treaty.

Finally, we must preserve superior military technologies and a healthy industrial base, enabling us to reconstitute much larger forces if a major hostile power were to begin to emerge in Europe or Asia. The impact on defense industries must be a factor in decisions on whether or not to acquire new weapons systems and the pace of procurement. This impact must also be considered in shaping other kinds of policies, like restrictions on arms sales abroad, which could cut further into industrial capability. Moreover there is overcapacity in the defense industries of the Western nations and other major countries. Given all these complexities it would be helpful to begin discussions aimed at rationalizing defense industrial capabilities in Europe, North America and East Asia and coordinating arms transfer policies.

The United States can clearly now afford to make substantial cuts in its armed forces and military spending. President Bush has already proposed to cut U.S. forces by about 25 percent over the next six years. Leading defense experts in the Congress have proposed somewhat deeper reductions.

The Bush Administration's defense budget proposal would reduce military spending by nearly 20 percent, in real terms, by fiscal 1997, reducing it from about $280 to $230 billion in 1992 dollars. Overall, the defense burden would decline from the more than 6 percent of GNP that characterized the Reagan years to about 3.4 percent, a level not seen since before World War II. In other words, under the Administration's program, about three percent of the nation's output would be shifted from defense to different purposes over a ten-year period.

The Commission had neither the resources nor the time to carry out the analyses required to reach a detailed judgment on the size and structure of U.S. armed forces for the post-Cold War era. Most, but not all of us, have concluded that the United States can make even deeper cuts in defense spending than those proposed thus far by the Administration without jeopardizing American security, thereby freeing even more resources for pressing domestic needs or for other international programs.

We all agree that care must be exercised in the pace with which reductions are implemented. Cut too rapidly into defense investments, and our technological superiority and industrial base could be eroded. Cut too rapidly into personnel, and U.S. forces could be too small to play a global role when contingencies arise. Too fast a pace of reductions would also spell hardships for the men and women in uniform, as well as for defense workers, companies and whole communities.

Strengthening Collective Security through the United Nations

The collective security system described in the U.N. Charter was stymied by the Cold War. Collective security has now come of age. Although it is not yet (and may never) become the sophisticated system originally envisaged, collective security has shown renewed potential in a variety of regional disputes around the globe. After all, the world recently witnessed how a U.S.-led coalition authorized by the U.N. Security Council won the Gulf War.

U.N. peacekeeping forces have been increasingly relied upon to end armed conflicts between and within states that neither the United States nor any of its allies were prepared to take on alone. As of mid-1992 U.N. forces were engaged in a dozen operations. Peacekeeping forces now monitor disengagement agreements, supervise elections, disarm hostile factions and even administer territories in dispute. U.N. guard forces are being deployed in greater numbers to protect relief workers in dangerous environments. Special U.N. envoys are being dispatched more often to mediate disputes.

Table 8: U.N. Peacekeeping Operations

(As of April 1992)

Location	Date Deployed	Annual Cost (Million U.S.$)	Troop Strength
Israel	1948	31	300
India/Pakistan	1949	5	39
Cyprus	1964	31[1]	2,200
Golan Heights	1974	43	1,330
Lebanon	1978	157	5,800
Iraq/Kuwait	1991	67	500
Angola	1991	110[2]	840
El Salvador	1991	59[3]	1,150
Western Sahara	1991	59	375
Yugoslavia	1992	607	14,370
Cambodia	1992	1,900[4]	15-20,000
Somalia	1992	23[5]	550

Source: United Nations
Note: The United Nations anticipates an increase in peacekeeping assessments from U.S.$ 421 million in 1991 to U.S.$ 2.7 billion in 1992.

[1] Funded by voluntary contributions rather than assessments against U.N. members.

[2] Total cost from 1 June 1991 to 31 October 1992.

[3] From 1 January 1992 to 31 October 1992.

[4] From 15 March 1992 to 14 June 1993.

[5] From April 1992 to October 1992.

In all of these activities, American leadership can play a critical role in galvanizing collective endeavors for challenges that simply cannot be ignored or managed unilaterally. We will inevitably rely more and more on collective security to cope with new military challenges – or they will not be dealt with at all.

A strong commitment to collective security does not infringe on our ability and right to take justifiable unilateral actions. The U.N. Charter explicitly recognizes that all nations have an inherent right of self-defense. In this respect, the U.N.'s founders were realistic about the limitations of any multilateral organization. To protect the national interest America will always preserve the right to act unilaterally. But we should also recognize that collective security enhances, not constrains, our strength and flexibility. Collective action is the most effective response to the kinds of threats we are likely to face.

We can strengthen the United Nations' ability to enforce collective security with broad reforms in the structure of the Security Council, the roles of U.N. agencies, the powers and resources of the Secretary-General and the organization and practices of the Secretariat.

But much more can be done short of fundamental reform to strengthen the U.N.'s contribution to world peace. As a first step we must bolster the U.N.'s ability to carry out peacekeeping operations. Peacekeeping duties are expanding rapidly and it takes near-Herculean efforts on the part of U.N. personnel to meet the financial and logistical burdens of daily operations.

To accomplish their missions, U.N. peacekeepers are increasingly being asked to move into dangerous territory. But the procedures by which the U.N. prepares for and carries out peacekeeping tasks are cobbled anew with each mission. Funds must be raised at the beginning of each operation, and full funding is rarely obtained from member states on schedule. Contributions are assessed on the basis of a special formula, which imposes disproportionate burdens on the United States and on other permanent members of the Security Council.

Table 9: 1992 UN Assessments

Regular and Peacekeeping

Country	Regular Budget Contributions[1] (Millions US$)	% of U.N. Budget	Peacekeeping Contributions[2] (Millions US$)	% of Peacekeeping Budget[3]
US	298.6	25.00	810.8	30.38
Japan	122.6	12.45	332.3	12.45
Russian Fed.	92.7	9.41	305.1	11.43
Germany	87.9	8.93	238.3	8.93
France	59.1	6.00	194.6	7.29
UK	49.4	5.02	162.8	6.10
Canada	30.7	3.11	83.0	3.11
Spain	19.5	1.98	52.9	1.98
Brazil	15.7	1.59	42.4	1.59
Australia	14.9	1.51	40.3	1.51

Source:
United Nations

[1] This includes neither outstanding contributions from previous years nor the 1992 peacekeeping assessments.

[2] Based on the Secretary General's 1992 estimated total peacekeeping budget of U.S.$ 2.7 billion, less U.S.$ 31 million for the Cyprus Force, which is voluntarily funded.

[3] The five permanent members of the Security Council are assessed at a higher rate for peacekeeping than regular U.N. members.

This ad hoc approach has often restricted the scope of U.N. peacekeeping missions, and sometimes delayed them to a point of near-disaster. If U.N. peacekeepers are to face greater dangers, they must be organized more professionally, be better trained and equipped and be supported like the world-class force they are intended to be.

To do this, the international community should first match resources to its rhetoric. We propose making peacekeeping a part of the regular U.N. budget, and assessing each nation's contribution on the basis of the same formula used for other regular U.N. expenses.

As stated earlier this would reduce the U.S. share of peacekeeping costs. We also endorse the establishment of a special fund to generate emergency operating monies for U.N. peacekeeping operations. Such a fund would give the Secretary-General more leeway in getting a mission started, thereby avoiding troublesome delays.

The United States should fund its U.N. peacekeeping obligations from the Defense Department budget – not the State Department budget. These operations are properly a major contribution to our security. Congress may be more willing to allocate Defense Department funds for peacekeeping assessments than it has been to appropriate funds from the strapped State Department budget.

Countries should also predesignate units that they might be prepared to commit for peacekeeping missions and provide them the specialized training necessary. The United States must accept this responsibility as well. The U.N. planning staff itself should be strengthened with officers seconded from national military organizations.

Of course, all this will require money. But even if the cost of peacekeeping were to increase tenfold from the almost half a billion dollars of 1991, it would still be a bargain. After all, the war against Iraq cost tens of billions of dollars. If U.N. peacekeepers had been stationed on the border of Kuwait before the Iraqi invasion, blood might not have been shed nor world treasure lost.

Americans need to understand that U.N. peacekeeping has become an important asset to our own security. It brings stability to conflicts that, if left untended, can spiral out of control and directly threaten our allies and our interests overseas.

In addition to peacekeeping, the United Nations must take steps to prepare better for military enforcement actions.

The U.N. Charter prefers diplomatic and economic instruments and envisions military action only as a weapon of last resort to maintain or restore peace. But if collective security is to be taken seriously, the U.N. must be prepared, in the end, to use force.

Strengthening the U.N.'s ability to use force to end conflicts is a much more difficult assignment than preparing for peacekeeping. Since this would expose U.N. personnel to much greater danger it will involve tough political decisions by member governments in each case. We recommend that discussions commence among the permanent members of the Security Council and other states to examine the feasibility of concluding the standby force agreements required by Article 43 of the U.N. Charter.

The U.N. Participation Act of 1945 long ago established the legal basis for U.S. participation in such standby arrangements. Participating states would designate a number of military units that would be assigned on a case-by-case basis to U.N. enforcement actions at the request of the Security Council; the United States, of course, would retain its power to veto any Security Council decision. America and some other nations may hesitate to sign standby agreements today. But the need for such a U.N. force has become increasingly apparent. We should move in that direction.

We note that the U.N. Secretary-General's recent report, *An Agenda for Peace*, contains detailed proposals to strengthen the U.N. collective security system. We urge the Administration and Congress to give serious attention to the Secretary-General's recommendations.

Regional Collective Security Organizations

Issues the world community could never resolve are often effectively addressed by countries in a single region. Europe is farthest along in this respect, but there have been signs of renewed life for collective regional security arrangements in East Asia, South Asia and Latin America.

The CSCE is emerging as a primary, though not exclusive, institutional vehicle through which the Atlantic community of states can manage change in the new Europe. The CSCE has a good record of setting norms and monitoring changes in the behavior of states. It is based on an excellent set of principles of international behavior and can be a useful protector of individual liberties.

Under CSCE auspices, member nations have agreed to intrusive verification and arms control arrangements. The United States and our democratic allies could use the CSCE to resolve nationalist tensions, prevent gross violations of human rights and defuse crises.

The CSCE has notable shortcomings. Its legitimacy and power are limited because it is based not on a treaty, but on informal agreements. Until recently, the CSCE has worked exclusively on the unanimity principle and, with more than fifty members, the organization is too unwieldy to become quickly a collective defense organization. Thus far it has been unable to act decisively in a crisis.

The Commission believes that a strengthened CSCE could contribute importantly to European security. If the shortcomings just listed were corrected over time, the organization could evolve into an institution with the means to enforce the norms of behavior to which member nations, including Soviet and Yugoslav successor states, have committed themselves. Holding member nations and militant groups within those nations accountable for their actions could help defuse ethnic conflicts and prevent their spillover across borders. The CSCE could move into new areas of arms reductions and verification, mediation and early warning mechanisms, and crisis prevention and management.[1]

---

[1] Mr. Carlucci believes this paragraph overstates the CSCE's potential.

Strengthening the CSCE would not weaken NATO. The two can operate side by side. Each requires energetic American engagement; neither requires an extensive American troop presence. The U.S. and European nations should retain flexibility, prepared to earmark national forces for peacekeeping missions under direct U.N. or CSCE auspices. The main burden of European defense and collective security, however, must rest with the Europeans.

In the *Western Hemisphere,* traditional threat perceptions that shaped U.S. policy have lost their relevance. Most nations in our hemisphere are beginning to embrace democracy and free-market economic policies, providing new common interests. While still apprehensive about our throwing our weight around, Latin American nations have reached out to the United States in an awareness that we and the West generally are now the only source of support for development. The result has been a new collegial "era of good feelings" which, among other things, has given a lease on life to the Organization of American States (OAS).

By the end of the 1980s, the OAS had degenerated into a debating forum, to which fewer and fewer substantive issues were brought. The sudden new convergence of values and concerns has sparked a revival of interest in the OAS. The organization has now begun to take up a broad agenda.

While many of the issues on this agenda – narcotics, terrorism, environment, migration and refugees, social instability, human rights, Haiti – have clear security considerations, the U.S. strategic interest in Latin America has become largely economic in nature. Indeed the stability, well-being and security of these nations will rest on progress toward economic prosperity and social justice. Their economic growth will also lead to more trade and more jobs in the United States.

Much remains to be done to improve OAS effectiveness. The use of military or other instruments to support peacekeeping and the defense of democracy may prove necessary. But this will have to be approached carefully through intensive discussion and mutual consent.

In *East Asia and the Pacific,* the United States has relied on bilateral security commitments to protect its interests and to maintain regional stability. These arrangements have worked well and should be maintained and modified as regional and global circumstances change.

However, the Commission believes that the United States should also begin to encourage a multilateral forum for regional security consultations. Many long-standing barriers to normal relations and dialogue among Asian nations have fallen away in the aftermath of the Cold War. This regional forum should complement, not replace,

American bilateral security commitments and military deployments. Our goal should be to begin a regional process that will bring East Asia to a higher level of dialogue in security matters.[2]

In *Africa,* conditions for regional security are dismal. Vicious and bloody conflicts have become endemic in many African countries. No other region of the world has suffered more from war in recent years; no other region can afford it less.

The Organization of African Unity lacks the means to make Africa more secure although it is examining how such means could be created. The great powers, including the United States, have been reluctant to become engaged. The United Nations, which has been deeply involved in humanitarian relief in Africa for many years, has the greatest potential to improve the security of Africa. The United States should work to ensure that U.N. agencies are adequately funded to provide at least minimal levels of sustenance to the innocent victims of Africa's wars. Strengthening the U.N.'s peacekeeping capabilities as we recommend could also help quell violence in Africa.

Demilitarization

World military expenditures are already declining after a sharp rise that began in the late 1970s. As shown in Table 10, the peak occurred in 1988, when global military expenditures totaled nearly $1.2 trillion in current dollars. Because of sharply lower spending by the former Warsaw Pact countries, global military expenditures will fall below the trillion dollar level this year. If announced intentions are fulfilled, world military spending should fall below $800 billion by 1996.

The Commission believes the United States should work on a broad front to secure even deeper demilitarization. America can lead by helping resolve regional conflicts. When peace is established, defense cuts follow naturally – witness the decline in Egyptian and Israeli military spending since the Camp David Accords. Over time the strengthening of U.N. and regional collective security procedures and forces can help assure states that their vital interests will be protected without the use of excessive resources for defense.

Weapons are mostly a result, not a root cause, of conflict. But if we can check the cycle of arms competition – a cycle of acquisition, suspicion, deployment and war – the task of mediators and diplomats will be that much easier. Moreover, military spending remains an undue burden throughout the developing world, hampering economic development and social and political advancement.

---

[2] Mr. Carlucci believes that it would be premature for the U.S. to encourage a multilateral forum for regional security consultations.

Table 10: Military Expenditures

(Billions of Constant 1992 Dollars)

	1980	1988	1989	1990	1991	1992	1996
U.S.[a]	233	326	328	312	325	311	230[e]
Other Members of NATO[b]	157	177	179	194	196	190[e]	170[e]
Soviet Successor States[c]	327	370	348	325	307	150[f]	100[f]
Former Members of the Warsaw Pact[d]	55	64	61	52[e]	32[e]	30[e]	25[e]
Japan[b]	21	32	32	33	34	36[e]	35[e]
China[d]	27	25	25	24	24	26[e]	30[e]
Saudi Arabia[d]	25	16	17	18	19[g]	20[g]	25[e]
All Others[d]	167	166	158	178	180	180	175
Total	**1012**	**1176**	**1148**	**1136**	**1107**	**943**	**790**

Sources
a. Secretary of Defense, Annual Reports to Congress, various years.
b. *Report on Allied Contributions to the Common Defense*, various years.
c. Defense Intelligence Agency Testimony, Allocation of Resources in the Soviet Union and China, various years.
d. World Military Expenditures and Arms Transfers, Arms Control and Disarmament Agency, 1990.
e. Defense Forecasts, Inc.
f. Based on Lt. General James R. Clapper Jr.'s testimony before the Senate Armed Services Committee on Jan. 22, 1992.
g. Saudi Press Agency, Riyadh.

As part of this demilitarization policy, we must also reverse the trend toward more and more nations gaining access to weapons of mass destruction and the means to deliver them. Across a wide swath of Asia, from the Levant to the Persian Gulf to South Asia to the Korean Peninsula, nations are racing to acquire nuclear, chemical and even biological weapons. Dozens of states are also acquiring longer-range missiles and aircraft to deliver these weapons of mass destruction. The United States and the Soviet Union – whose rivalry was based on abstract ideological conflict – came to the brink of nuclear war. What, then, are the prospects for restraint between nations that harbor ancient fears and centuries-old feuds?

Demilitarization and stemming nuclear proliferation should be key American goals. Toward these ends, the Commission envisions a long-term approach:

One: Work to reduce global acquisitions of conventional weapons and the size of armed forces.

The United States and its partners should establish the goal of cutting world military expenditures to $600 billion, in today's prices, by the beginning of the new century – slashing in half the peak expenditure level reached in 1988. This objective can only be accomplished by working to create an international environment in which states can place their trust in collective security. Also, as noted previously, the rationalization of worldwide arms production will be crucial to cutting military spending.

We must, of course, ensure that the new states of the former Soviet Union and the nations of Eastern Europe fulfill their plans to scale back greatly defense spending and reduce their military production. Their urgent needs for Western capital, technology and goodwill provide us tremendous leverage to accomplish this goal.

Western Europe's military expenditures are just beginning to drop significantly. If the former Soviet Union's military establishment continues to be dismantled to the extent that now seems likely, we should expect the West Europeans to join us in continuing to cut defense spending, freeing resources for domestic uses and for international programs.

East Asia's growing arms purchases may eventually slow with the diminishing threat from the former Soviet Union, though this is by no means certain. In years past the United States has urged Japan to boost its spending on defense. With the end of the Soviet threat, such pressure is no longer necessary or wise. Fear of Japan's military potential could ignite higher spending levels throughout the region. We should instead urge all the states of the region, most of which have major military modernization programs, to slow them down.

In the Middle East, arms expenditures are expected to rise, less because of the Arab-Israeli dispute than conflicting ambitions in the Persian Gulf. The new availability of inexpensive military equipment from the former Soviet Union raises the risk of a massive infusion of arms into the region, and particularly to Iran. Fearing this possibility, Saudi Arabia and other Western-oriented nations are seeking to purchase large quantities of American and European armaments. The possibility of lower defense spending in the Persian Gulf will thus be linked closely to the success or failure of efforts to bring about a less threatening government in Iraq, to reintegrate Iran into the peaceful community of nations and to persuade the Soviet successor states to restrain their military exports.

In the end the best incentives for encouraging many countries to reduce military spending might be financial. Only in the past year have major lending nations and multilateral agencies indicated that they would consider the level of national defense spending when reviewing requests by developing countries for financial assistance. This is a welcome development.

The United States and other major national and multilateral contributors should move to make this linkage to military spending a regular feature of foreign assistance policy. Japan has already taken steps in this direction. In view of the overcapacity in Western defense industries, and the demilitarization goal, it is particularly important that the building of arms industries in developing nations – often a goal of armament policies – be discouraged.

Finally, we must continue to strive to reduce arms transfers, especially sales of advanced weapons that can spark greater arms competitions in unstable portions of the globe. The recent establishment of a conventional arms registry at the United Nations is an important step toward restraining arms sales. This voluntary reporting system ultimately should become mandatory, and the United States should lead in that direction.

Since the Gulf War the five permanent members of the Security Council have agreed on guidelines for the transfers of arms to the Middle East. But these principles are too vague to make a dent in the global arms traffic. Continuing negotiations are necessary to add greater specificity to their criteria and to outline their application in specific regions. Curbing arms sales is difficult for political and economic reasons; if this goal is to be achieved, all major suppliers, particularly the United States, must be serious in its pursuit. As a first step the big five suppliers need to agree on ways to consult on a confidential basis *before* arms sales are concluded, so that prospective transfers that trouble other countries might be withdrawn.

The rueful history of efforts to limit arms, however, teaches us that restraints that depend solely on supplier cartels are doomed to failure. As with the war on drugs, we also need to focus on the demand side. At their root arms transfers reflect international conflicts. Supplier restraints treat the symptoms, but they do not deal with the underlying causes. For this regional diplomacy and U.N. peacekeeping are essential.

Two: Strengthen efforts to constrain weapons of mass destruction.

The proliferation of weapons of mass destruction is the greatest single threat to American security. Despite many successes the non-proliferation effort remains uneven and at risk.

The dramatic agreement in June 1992 by Presidents George Bush and Boris Yeltsin will drastically reduce the two states' nuclear inventories. The agreement is unprecedented both in the scope of its provisions and the rapidity with which it was negotiated. Once implemented, the agreement will have reduced the two nations' strategic inventories by about 70 percent from their levels prior to last year's START agreement. Perhaps more important, the new agreement calls for the complete elimination of the most threatening weapons on the two sides: land-based missiles with multiple independently targetable warheads.

We congratulate the two presidents on this accomplishment and urge them and their successors to place the highest priority on the completion and timely implementation of the agreement.

This accord has changed the context for our non-proliferation efforts. Now America must work to deepen and broaden reductions in nuclear weapon inventories in the Soviet successor states. Political control of nuclear weapons – indeed, political stability itself – is uncertain in the former Soviet Union. It is essential that no new nuclear powers be permitted to emerge among the successor states. We must drive home this point and back up our demands by offering the money, equipment and expertise to help Russia fulfill its commitments to destroy weapons transferred from the other new states on whose territory they still are located – Belarus, Kazakhstan and Ukraine. We must continue efforts to prevent nuclear scientists and engineers from the former Soviet Union from becoming a brain trust for rogue states with nuclear ambitions.

The United States is also now in a better position to press for broader negotiations with the declared nuclear powers – Russia, China, Britain and France. The latter three nations have always conditioned their participation in nuclear arms talks on deep cuts in superpowers' nuclear arsenals. With the planned near-elimination of U.S. and Russian tactical nuclear weapons, announced in reciprocal statements in 1991, and now the agreement on deep cuts in strategic nuclear forces, this stated prerequisite has been satisfied. While objections may be mounted by the other three, we should persevere in seeking the prompt start of five-power talks on the future of nuclear arsenals.

Given the projected deep reductions in our nuclear stocks, we now need to determine what levels we should seek in the arsenals of others to protect our political and security interests.

The U.S.-Russian agreement on deep cuts in nuclear weapons also puts America, working with others, in a stronger position to extend indefinitely and strengthen the Non-Proliferation Treaty at the 1995 review conference. Prospects for a stronger non-proliferation regime emerging from the conference would be further improved if the other declared nuclear powers were reducing their stocks.

It is especially important to bolster the key monitoring organization in nuclear trade, the International Atomic Energy Agency (IAEA), which in the past has been starved for resources and unable to exercise its full mandate.

The IAEA is a creature of the community of nations. It can do only what nations, and particularly the major powers, are willing to permit it to do. The IAEA's budget, flat for years, should be increased substantially to strengthen its ability to safeguard nuclear facilities and to promote peaceful uses of nuclear energy. Among other purposes the money should be used to expand the staff of the organization and to train IAEA inspectors in the wider range of tasks now required of the organization. The organization should also be given access to new technologies to strengthen its capability to monitor nuclear sites. And the IAEA should be encouraged by the major powers to execute its inspection powers to the fullest, challenging undeclared facilities in signatory countries. In support of this task, nations should share information with the organization on a routine basis. Practical steps, such as the issuance of permanent global visas to inspectors to avoid disabling delays, also should be undertaken.

The shocking scope of the Iraqi nuclear program reveals the extent to which various governments have in the past turned a blind eye to national firms that make a mockery of guidelines governing nuclear exports, particularly those pertaining to dual-use technologies. The twenty-seven countries of the Nuclear Suppliers Group have adopted strict export control measures governing dual-use technology. What is now needed is a tough-minded campaign to enforce adherence to these guidelines with uniform and severe financial and criminal penalties for violators – both the sellers and the recipients.

The Security Council declared in January 1992 that the spread of weapons of mass destruction constitutes a threat to peace and security. This opens the way to mandatory sanctions.

The Commission believes that the use of military force to prevent nuclear proliferation must be retained as an option of last resort. In some cases, as in North Korea, the acquisition of nuclear capabilities could completely destabilize a region, raising grave threats to international peace. Whenever possible we should act collectively. But we must be prepared to act on our own.

Nuclear Testing

The dismantlement of the Soviet Union raises anew the possibility of further constraints on the development of nuclear weapons and on nuclear testing. The United States has already stopped the production of special nuclear materials and new nuclear warheads, and the President's defense program for fiscal 1993-97 indicates the termination of all major programs to modernize nuclear forces other than the Trident II missile. The former Soviet Union has not tested a nuclear weapon for nearly two years, and Russian production of nuclear weapons and materials appears to have been cut back substantially. France has announced a limited test moratorium, China holds an average of one nuclear test a year. Britain's testing is performed as part of the U.S. program.

This situation suggests the possibility of an agreement to greatly reduce nuclear testing. The Commission discussed this question at length, but did not reach agreement.

Some Commissioners believe it is no longer necessary to develop new types of nuclear weapons. The only tests needed, they maintain, are the very few intended to ensure the continued safety and reliability of nuclear weapons.

These Commissioners believe that the United States should take advantage of this situation to arrange with the other nuclear powers a moratorium on all nuclear tests and to use that period to negotiate a treaty that tightly constrains nuclear testing forever. Such an agreement might permit each declared nuclear power to carry out only one test per year and place much tighter limits on the permitted explosive yields of such tests than those now enshrined in the existing Threshold Test Ban Treaty. Any such treaty, they note, must also include effective means of verifying compliance. The technical means to provide such verification with high confidence are available.

The primary reason for this initiative, these Commissioners believe, is to strengthen U.S. efforts to limit nuclear proliferation. By making clear in this way that it no longer intends to develop new types of nuclear weapons, the United States would greatly strengthen its efforts to persuade other nations to adhere to the Non-Proliferation Treaty, strengthen and extend that treaty and otherwise restrain nuclear proliferation.

Other Commissioners believe that as long as the United States relies on nuclear weapons, some testing is necessary to improve the safety of warheads, to maintain capabilities in the physics of weapons, and to maintain confidence in the reliability of the stockpile. They note America may again find it desirable to develop new warhead designs and may want to test for that purpose. In any event the changing world makes it appropriate to consider whether fewer tests are required and lower limits on the permissible yields of tests might be acceptable. Under some circumstances, moreover, the United States might consider temporary pauses in testing in pursuit of specific international political objectives, such as helping Russia persuade other former Soviet republics to give up nuclear weapons on their territory.

These Commissioners oppose a prolonged moratorium on nuclear testing, however, and see no advantage in a treaty that would greatly constrain nuclear tests. They specifically reject the proposition that constraints on U.S. nuclear testing would strengthen U.S. efforts to limit the proliferation of nuclear weapons and point out that several nations – Israel, Pakistan and South Africa – are believed to have acquired nuclear weapons capabilities without crossing the bright line of testing.

Other Concerns

Nuclear weapons, of course, are not our only concern. As a key part of our effort to constrain weapons of mass destruction, we must also address the issues of chemical and biological weapons, missiles and missile technology.

- Long-range and intermediate-range missiles are useful only for offensive military operations or as terror weapons for use against cities. The fledgling Missile Technology Control Regime, designed to limit exports of missiles and missile-related technologies, should be broadened to include more countries and strengthened by defining tighter constraints on components and supporting technologies.

- The Commission urges fast completion of a comprehensive ban on chemical weapons, as well as diplomatic efforts by the United States and other countries to persuade as many nations as possible to subscribe to it. The signatories should pledge to protect any nation attacked by chemical weapons. Ridding the world of chemical weapons will be extremely difficult, if possible at all. Verifying any such prohibition is particularly hard, requiring highly intrusive inspection procedures.

- The Biological Weapons Treaty needs to be strengthened. This will be the most difficult agreement of all to police. An inspection regime could be developed based on the Chemical Weapons Treaty, although cheating would be even harder to detect. Signatory nations should press all others to sign and ratify the Biological Weapons Treaty.

Future Questions

The Commission discussed extensively the prospect of working to eliminate, progressively, weapons of mass destruction from the face of the earth. The bulk of the Commission concluded that while such a goal might be desirable, it is simply not feasible. Nuclear weapons technology cannot be disinvented just because the world has changed. But the new world does provide us the opportunity to reconsider the future roles and requirements of nuclear weapons.

Some basic questions have to be examined. What objectives are now served by U.S. nuclear weapons – and what threats are posed by other countries? How many nuclear weapons would we need for deterrence – and what do we seek to deter? Do we need nuclear weapons over the long term, for example, to offset Chinese conventional forces? What is the role of defensive forces?

The June 1992 agreement between Russia and the United States prompts us to think anew about these questions. It accomplished in months what twenty years of detailed negotiations found impossible even to consider: drastic cuts in weapon inventories and the complete elimination of the most destabilizing systems. This achievement came about not because of any innovation in negotiation technique or style, but because the conflict that spawned such weapons has vanished.

The June agreement brings home an essential point: we may be able to reduce radically weapons of mass destruction, but greater progress toward the durable peace we seek will come from tackling the root causes of conflict such weapons manifest. The experience of the great democracies can be a guide. Although the English and the French were mortal enemies for a thousand years, Shakespeare's fond wish "that never war advance his bleeding sword 'twixt England and fair France" is now a fact so ordinary that it goes unnoticed. Free, properous nations simply do not seek war. Nor do British and French nuclear weapons threaten America. As more countries join the widening circle of democracy, so grows the circle of trust.

A secure peace is obviously not the work of a few years. It could well be the work of a whole century, the twenty-first century. But we should not condemn our descendants to live forever under the shadow of Armageddon. The time to start finding solutions is now.

"Without internal peace, that is peace among citizens and between the citizens and the state, there can be no guarantee of external peace: a state that ignores the will and the rights of its citizens can offer no guarantee that it will respect the will and the rights of other peoples, nations, and states .... A lasting peace and disarmament can only be the work of free people."

Vaclav Havel

"Without internal peace, that is peace among citizens and between the citizens and the state, there can be no guarantee of external peace: a state that ignores the will and the rights of its citizens can offer no guarantee that it will respect the will and the rights of other peoples, nations, and states .... A lasting peace and disarmament can only be the work of free people."

Vaclav Havel

VI. Toward a Freer World

Democracy was once the ideal of a handful of nations. It is now – for the first time in history – the way in which a majority of the world's nations govern themselves. At a time when Communism has imploded and the information revolution has spread freedom's values, democracy is spreading as the most desirable, credible and resilient form of government.

When we speak of "democracy," we are, of course, describing a political ethos and way of life that can vary significantly from one society to the next. The American brand is perhaps unique. It would be arrogant to seek its replication among different peoples and cultures. Each society must find its own path.

What then is democracy? The variety of democratic systems is formidable, but all democracies share certain core values and characteristics. A democratic society is one where the rule of law not only prevails, but is based upon the informed consent of the people. Political leaders are chosen in fair and periodic elections in which an opposition has an honest opportunity to win. All adult citizens, regardless of gender or color or religion, are eligible to vote. Individuals can speak, publish, assemble and organize freely. Free and independent trade unions exist.

In recent years a growing international consensus on these and other attributes of democracy has emerged. In various declarations the United Nations, the Conference on Security and Cooperation in Europe and other organizations have defined democracy and pledged to promote it.

America's Interests in Democracy

Why should Americans care about democratization elsewhere in the world? The Commission believes that the promotion of democracy is a worthy goal in itself. But there are strong reasons why the spread of democracy is in our self-interest.

- **National security:** Democracy is based upon the consent of the people through their elected representatives, and few today entertain illusions about the nature of modern war. History teaches us that democratic societies do not attack one another. What more fundamental contributions to our security have there been than the realization of long-suppressed democratic aspirations in Eastern Europe? Thanks to the Havels and Walesas, the West no longer needs to plan for a major war in Europe.

- **Economic self-interest:** Stable democracies are generally better trade and investment partners than repressive regimes. While new democracies may need foreign assistance to "jump-start" their economies, such investments will over the long term benefit the American economy as well. And the cost of promoting democracy comes cheaply compared to the colossal sums that we spent to defend against totalitarianism.

- **Environmental goals:** The pressures for environmental reform originated in democratic nations where citizens could force changes in government policies. It is no coincidence that the most egregious assaults on the environment – Chernobyl and the ruin of the Aral Sea – occurred under Communist rule in the former Soviet empire.

- **Human rights:** Recent U.S. administrations, liberal and conservative, have with varying emphasis put human rights on our foreign policy agenda. Respect for the individual is a core American value. Only free governments and societies are vigilant in protecting the rights of their citizens. We do not see refugees from democratic nations.

For these reasons the promotion of democracy deserves and enjoys the support of the American people. Expanding freedom provides one of the central pillars of our foreign policy. Moreover the end of our global rivalry with the Soviet Union sharply reduces the need to muffle our concerns about unsavory governments because of security concerns.

Challenges to Democracy

New democracies are born in euphoria. But democracy is not easy. Political consensus is almost always eroded by disagreement over economic policies. Elected leaders can be corrupt or incompetent. Persistent poverty can devastate democracies. And we have seen how ethnic and national feuds can overwhelm democratic institutions.

Elsewhere in the world cultural and ideological factors hold back the growth of freedom. Aspects of Islamic fundamentalism, particularly its treatment of women, appear incompatible with democracy. However, we should not give up on efforts to draw Islamic movements into the democratic community. Economic growth, the rise of a middle class and integration into the world economy will foster the evolution of democratic institutions in poorer Islamic countries.

The participation of fundamentalists in democratic processes may well open the door to Islamic totalitarian rule. But once we oppose the results of free elections where they do not produce the results we want, we are heading toward subjective judgments and away from the often frustrating application of democratic standards. If a fundamentalist group wins power and seeks to crush democracy, we could then join others to apply various measures to isolate it, looking toward the restoration of freedom.

There is no easy path through this thicket. We should be careful to distinguish between various forms of Islam and not mistake fundamentalism for a world ideological threat comparable to Communism. The capacity and will of the United States to check its spread will be limited. The essential task will fall to the leaders and peoples of the countries concerned.

Communist regimes continue to prevent the emergence of democracy for the more than one billion people in China, North Korea, Vietnam and Cuba. Repressive non-Communist governments hold sway in many parts of the Middle East, Africa and Asia. For each of these countries, the United States should pursue a realistic strategy. We will need to balance our other interests and the local context. We can conduct necessary business without coddling repressive regimes or abandoning support for human rights and political freedom.

In these cases the Commission supports a tailored approach that would include trade and investment to promote economic reforms and market-oriented systems. Increasing economic opportunity stimulates pressures for democracy, and greater prosperity helps it survive. Trade and investment can quietly help undermine unjust regimes, while we use diplomatic channels and public statements to send a clear political message.

Assets for Democracies

Americans have two powerful allies in building democracy – the world media and the world democratic community.

Democracy is nurtured and sustained by the free flow of information among peoples. The contributions of Radio Free Europe, Radio Liberty and the Voice of America, as well as European media such as the British Broadcasting Corporation and Deutsche Welle, were invaluable in disseminating information and hope behind the Iron Curtain. We also witnessed how televised images helped shatter one Communist regime after another, like glasses before a resounding pitch. Peoples no longer see the world through the distorted images manufactured by regimes; they compare their fate with that of others around the globe.

In the past individuals could not look to the world community to legitimize or protect a "right" to democratic governance. Now an emerging global commitment to democracy has become a guiding principle in the work of the Conference on Security and Cooperation in Europe, the United Nations, the Organization of American States, the European Community and international financial institutions. Many of these bodies are now involved in election and human-rights monitoring and in helping create and consolidate democratic governments. We need not act alone in an American crusade to promote freedom.

Multilateral organizations bring the pooled authority of many states to the advancement of democracy. The United States may in certain instances still need to act unilaterally. But, whenever possible, we should engage other nations and collective institutions.

Some of the most effective work in the cause of democracy today is being carried out by private and nongovernmental organizations, such as the National Endowment for Democracy. These groups help strengthen democracy where it has emerged. They also have the flexibility and independence to encourage democratic activity in repressed societies where it is often difficult for the U.S. government to do so.

Building Blocks

Democracy, like other elements of our foreign policy, begins at home. The United States continues to struggle to reconcile diversity and unity, to sustain habits of cooperation while protecting the rights of individuals and groups to be different. This is a global challenge that America, despite serious flaws, has confronted better than any other society. Improving our society is the foundation for our efforts around the globe.

Where democratic breakthroughs have occurred, we should make major efforts to consolidate them. They include not only diplomacy and technical assistance, but also substantial public and private resources. America is committed to promoting democracy in Eastern Europe and the Soviet successor states. Giving priority to this task has its advantages. A targeted approach can make resources available efficiently and effectively. Moreover, success stories in one country can boost the morale and prospects of those struggling elsewhere for freedom. Conversely, failures can embolden totalitarian and authoritarian regimes.

But too much emphasis on selective democratization overlooks the increasingly universal character of democratization after the Cold War. No nation is excluded from democracy by culture or history. None should be deprived of it for lack of international support.

Furthermore, an overly selective approach would miss an historic opportunity to advance democracy in a large number of countries outside Eastern Europe and the former Soviet Union. Struggling democrats in Africa, Asia and Latin America also need America's backing and that of other democracies and multilateral organizations.

For decades American labor has been on the cutting edge of this global effort. Independent trade union movements remain precarious enterprises in many societies. They are critical to democratization. They give workers, so often exploited, basic rights of representation.

An American democratization strategy should include programs which develop political parties; assist in the administration and monitoring of fair elections; train parliamentarians, lawyers and judges; enhance the rule of law; build free trade unions; support independent media; cultivate open markets; aid private-sector institutions dedicated to human rights; and encourage political participation by all groups in society.

Complexities

Such an approach will require some hard choices.

Tensions will sometimes occur between democracy and self-determination. Demands for self-determination are erupting all over the world. This aspiration strikes a responsive chord in the United States. But sometimes the process narrows rather than broadens human rights. It has often promoted territorial exclusiveness for one ethnic group rather than the continuation or creation of a multiethnic state.

The complexities are enormous. Democratic systems alone do not always assure that ethnic concerns are protected. We should be sympathetic to expressions of self-determination but equally aware of its destructive potential. Our approach should be to help build conditions that will promote harmony between ethnic groups and protect individual and minority rights.

When democracy is assaulted, the U.S. response will vary with the circumstances. There will be times when the collapse of an elected government may be unavoidable. There will be times when international pressures on the takeover regime may inflict unacceptable hardships on the people. But as a general rule the United States should join other nations to impose punitive measures on countries whose democratic governments have been toppled by military coups or suspended by the national leadership.

Conclusion

In the new world, promoting democracy is more feasible and more important.

As with other complex issues there is no simple formula to fit every situation. We have proposed a strategy that includes several components – stronger democracy at home; a multilateral emphasis; support for private organizations; consistent public statements; full backing for the consolidation and restoration of democratic governments; and a case-by-case approach where democracy has yet to take root.

We should have no illusions. Fostering freedom around the world will be a long, arduous process with setbacks along the way. But we can now realistically hope there will be stable democracies throughout Eastern Europe, the Soviet successor states and the Western Hemisphere, with freedom spreading ever deeper into Asia and Africa. Such an expansion of the democratic community was unimaginable just five years ago.

We believe that history is on the side of freedom.

America is sauntering through her resources, and through the mazes of her politics with an easy nonchalance; but presently there will come a time… when she will be obliged to pull herself together, husband her resources, concentrate her strength, steady her methods, sober her views, restrict her vagaries, trust her best, not her average, members. That will be the time of change."

Woodrow Wilson

"America is sauntering through her resources, and through the mazes of her politics with an easy nonchalance; but presently there will come a time ... when she will be obliged to pull herself together, husband her resources, concentrate her strength, steady her methods, sober her views, restrict her vagaries, trust her best, not her average, members. That will be the time of change."

Woodrow Wilson

VII. Changing Our Ways

Proclamations of new epochs ring with the clarion call of a broken bell. Yet the more this Commission studied the shifting landscape, the more we became convinced that this is, indeed, a "time of change," – and a time of opportunity.

We find reassurance in the words of Oliver Wendell Holmes: "A thought is often original, though you have uttered it a hundred times. It has come to you over a new route, by a new and express train of associations."

We conclude where we began – foreign policy begins at home. We must make real for our own people the values we champion on the international scene even as we must manage our national resources in responsible fashion.

Changing our domestic ways also compels reexamination of our structures of government and our education for international affairs. For we are a country ill-equipped for new priorities. Our institutions creak with anachronisms. Many leaders proclaim change but act as if nothing has changed. And we are not preparing the next generation of Americans to understand, much less lead, in a transformed world.

The American constitutional system is not efficient for making policy, foreign or domestic. Nor did its founders intend it to be. Indeed the separation-of-powers often means a tug-of-war over public policy, especially when the President is of one party and Congress the other. Weak political parties, the power of television and money in campaigns and the heightened influence of special interests – these and other factors converge to test our capacity to deal with new priorities.

This Commission has strong faith in the resilience of the American people and institutions. This nation has surmounted crises far graver than our current predicament. Now we must find the political will to match our still ample resources. We must invest in our future rather than consume our inheritance.

To lead abroad we need to revamp the processes of government. There are fundamental challenges that both the executive and legislative branches must address:

- How can the government better integrate foreign and domestic concerns?

- Should it create new agencies, or restructure old ones, to reflect our growing stake in the world economy?

- How can we ensure that new priorities like the environment actually gain greater weight in decision making?

- Does the changed security climate permit a significant reduction in the tens of billions we spend on intelligence?

- Specifically, what changes should be considered in the National Security Council system in light of the above?

Another important issue is the relationship between the legislative and executive branches in the conduct of foreign policy. In recent years the executive has faced political, legal and even constitutional challenges regarding some of its actions in foreign affairs. Criticism has also been leveled at the ways in which Congress has fulfilled, or failed to fulfill, its own obligations. It is essential to examine how the two branches can better work out differences over foreign policy.

Such questions were beyond the mandate of this Commission. But our intensive deliberations repeatedly brought home their salience. We do not believe the answers can be left solely to the two branches of government. They need much wider public consideration.

As an unelected Commission, we shrink from recommending still another group. We have concluded, however, that these issues are so basic that they require a blue-ribbon panel made up of members of the legislative and executive branches and dedicated citizens from the private sector. Since governmental reorganization is always contentious, a bipartisan national commission would be of great value in forging consensus on the structural reforms that are needed.

To be sure, it will be the character and quality of people, not the adequacy of machinery, that will determine success.

Education, therefore, is indispensable to our efforts. The executive agencies and congressional staffs responsible for foreign policy must recruit and nurture professionals with fresh eyes, new expertise and a sharp appreciation for the melding of our internal and external interests. Equally important is that government service once again be seen as the honorable calling it is, not as the refuge of scoundrels feeding at the public trough.

Most fundamental is the learning of future generations. The new kind of American leadership we have outlined can only be advanced through persuasion and bargaining. It must rely on a sophisticated knowledge of the world and sensitivity to the perspectives of other nations.

Yet here too we are slighting our long-term interests. Our ranks are filled with experts better trained to deal with the past than the future. We must reorient university curricula and develop new cadres of professionals – not only for government but for business and finance, science and technology, culture and communications. And we must begin before college, imparting to children in elementary and secondary schools the necessary language skills and understanding of other peoples that our international role demands.

The new world is still in its infancy. Events will surprise us, as is history's habit in times of upheaval. In grappling with issues foreign and domestic, with the uncertainties of the moment and the dilemmas of the future, this Commission has concluded that simply altering our policies will not suffice.

"The release of atom power," Albert Einstein once noted, "changed everything except our way of thinking."

What troubled Einstein troubles us. We have to change our "way of thinking." About what is important. About making the most of our third chance. About our engagement abroad and renewal at home. About the promise for a richer, cleaner, safer and freer planet.

Changing our ways, America can lead such a world into the twenty-first century. □

The Carnegie Endowment National Commission on America and the New World

David R. Gergen

Editor-at-Large for *U.S. News and World Report*; political commentator for "The MacNeil/Lehrer Newshour;" former Communications Director in the White House.

William Gray

President, United Negro College Fund; former U.S. Congressman (D-Pennsylvania).

Richard Holbrooke

Managing Director, Lehman Brothers; former Assistant Secretary of State for East Asian and Pacific Affairs.

James T. Laney

President of Emory University; former Dean, Candler School of Theology, Emory University.

Jessica T. Mathews

Vice President of the World Resources Institute and columnist for *The Washington Post*; former Director of the Office of Global Issues on the staff of the National Security Council.

Alice M. Rivlin

Senior Fellow of the Brookings Institution; former Director of the Congressional Budget Office (CBO) and Assistant Secretary for Planning and Evaluation in the U.S. Department of Health, Education, and Welfare.

Paula Stern

President of the Stern Group; former Chairwoman and Commissioner of the International Trade Commission (ITC) ; former Senior Associate, Carnegie Endowment for International Peace.

Richard N. Perle

Resident Scholar, the American Enterprise Institute for Public Policy Research; former Assistant Secretary of Defense for International Security Policy.

James R. Schlesinger

Counsellor for the Center for Strategic and International Studies; Chairman of the Mitre Corporation and Senior Advisor, Lehman Brothers; former U.S. Secretary of Energy; former U.S. Secretary of Defense; former Director, Central Intelligence Agency.

Richard N. Perle and **James R. Schlesinger** participated in the deliberations of the Commission but chose not to associate themselves with the report.

Bill Moyers and **Condoleezza Rice** were original members of the Commission. Their schedules precluded their participation.

Commission Staff

Stephen Bosworth

Executive Director

Dan Hamilton

Coordinator

Barry Blechman
Charles Cooper
Mark Davis
Larry Fabian
David Scheffer

Senior Consultants

Barbara Bicksler
Nancy Blabey
Kevin Covert
Robin First
Shane Green
Liz Jasper
Kristin Ratnavale
Patricia Small